D0839687

What's In Your Box?

Designing the Life You Want

Dr. Linda L. Singh

Archway Publishing books may be ordered through booksellers or by contacting:

Archway Publishing
1663 Liberty Drive
Bloomington, IN 47403
www.archwaypublishing.com
844-669-3957

ISBN: 978-1-4808-9384-9 (sc)
ISBN: 978-1-4808-9383-2 (hc)
ISBN: 978-1-4808-9385-6 (e)

Library of Congress Control Number: 2020914217

Print information available on the last page.

Archway Publishing rev. date: 08/27/2020

I would like to thank many who inspired me in this journey. The first is several members of the Maryland National Guard. Without their support, encouragement and dedication, I would not have gotten the idea for this book. Janeen Birckhead and April Vogel, you two are simply amazing and were so encouraging and way too motivated when I talked with you about this concept. Now that it has come to fruition, thank you.

The Bosnia and Herzegovina country team for inviting me to the holiday gathering in December 2018. It was that event where I received, no stole the box from one of you during the gift exchange. It was more than just a box then and now it has created a new theory that I will use for years to come to help guide the dreams of many.

Lastly, I would like to thank my family for always supporting me in my crazy endeavors. Tara you were my tester of ideas and thoughts. Being an avid reader, you were the one who drove my creativity. Raj and Shaniece, you are always willing to listen and roll your eyes when things sounded too outlandish.

For the rest of the world, my goal is simple, I want to inspire you, challenge you to question your actions and behaviors, values and beliefs and intentions to determine if they are serving you well. If they are not, be bold, be brave and throw them out of your box, your life!

CONTENTS

CHAPTER I

The Meaning of a Box

On my grandmother's dresser sat a silver oval container that so intrigued me. It called to me. It was small and heavy, with a beautiful design on the top. It was a place where I could hide all kinds of small things.

This box hid my tiny secrets. To this day, it has a special place in my heart.

My grandmother has long since passed away, and my mother gave me that box, not knowing how much I loved it when I was younger. The moment she handed it to me, I was transported back in time. I remembered how important the box had been for me and how precious were the things I had kept in it. I still have the box, sitting in a place where I can see it every day. I don't have this treasure just as a keepsake but because it reminds me of valuable lessons I have learned over the years. I think the most important lesson I learned was how to protect things I value, while realizing that what I put in directly relates to what I get out.

This isn't the only box I have. Throughout my life, I have bought boxes for myself and given a lot of boxes as gifts. Each one of these boxes is beautiful and amazingly crafted in its own way.

As I think about my grandmother's box, all these years later, I can't help but realize that boxes have been a part of my life in so many ways. I loved to take cardboard boxes and make houses out of them. I had a blue box in which I kept my paper dolls, records, and writing books. As time went on and I started moving, I used boxes to pack those treasured items to get from one place to another.

I am sure many of you have put together keepsake boxes or promise boxes. Boxes are a part of our everyday lives in so many ways. Think about how you use boxes. You have boxes of food in your pantry. You have boxes to organize your office supplies and the things in your bathroom. You store your childhood mementos and the memories of your children in boxes. You keep important papers in fireproof boxes to keep them safe. You use boxes to safely transport things.

Yet it is a cliché these days to say we "think outside the box," as if a box is a negative thing, as if it confines us in some way and hems us in.

I challenge you to be open-minded when it comes to boxes. See boxes from a different perspective. They aren't just practical cubes you can throw things in for storage. They can be magical things that can transform your life, if you look at them in the right way.

WHAT IS THE BOX THEORY?

Before you can think out of the box, you have to start with a box.
—Twyla Tharp

What is the first thing that comes to mind when you think of a box? Do you see a hollow cube or something more mysterious? Do you see it as something that restricts or constrains you or something with infinite possibilities to be filled? If I asked you to use a box as a visual representation of your life, would you wonder if it would limit your imagination or your capacity to the dimensions of the box? The answer, of course, would depend on your approach and your perspective.

A box can be just a container in which to store things, but it can also be so much more.

A few years ago, I was talking to a group college sophomores. I asked them what they thought about when they looked at a box. I got a lot of different answers. Some thought a box was for storing junk; some thought it was a place to keep special objects safe. Another one answered that a box could be taken as a symbol that limits our abilities. There were a lot of answers, but none was in line with what I was about to tell them.

I said that a box can be a representation of your life. Just like a box may be full of precious things from different times and events, our lives are full of moments in time, where our goals and ambitions come alive. The size of the box is not important; the goals, dreams, and accomplishments we put into it are important. It's not about the box itself; it's about the contents of the box. What you fill it with is what matters.

I am not talking about the literal definition of a box. When I ask what's in your box, I'm not asking you about an actual box. Changing the way we think about boxes is foundational to the concepts that I will discuss in later chapters. Thinking about a physical box in an abstract manner, where the objects stored reflect your goals and accomplishments, is key. You must be intentional about the things that you place in your box, only placing things in there that you value or that represent your future.

When I asked the college students to consider the box as something more than a physical entity, their facial expressions showed their confusion. They weren't sure where the conversation was headed. Since I was there for a motivational-speaking session, the students were eager to know what my question was all about. Now that I had their attention, I shared the box theory with them.

What is the box theory? It is a metaphorical box, designed in a manner that represents your vision for your future. Think of it as a method for very intentionally designing, planning, committing, accomplishing, and celebrating your life. The box itself represents your future self. We are all different, so your box should be unique. You can use different materials for the physical box—cardboard, wood, metal, glass, or stone. You can decorate it in precious jewels, muted colors, or bright designs. There is no right or wrong; it only needs to be aligned with your vision and desires. It is an instrument that can be used to develop your ideas and refine them to an extent that you have a clearer vision of how to turn them into a reality.

I use a box because it represents security, protection, strength, and ownership. Unlike a bucket, which can easily be kicked over, a box provides a sturdier foundation and more space to place ideas, goals, and dreams, while reminding you that you must put in the work before you get something out. Our lives are so vast. It can be hard to grasp how to accomplish our goals and dreams. For many of us, it can be overwhelming to think about what we should be doing, whether what we are doing is right, or how we can know if we are doing what we really want to do.

As you will find in later chapters, the box theory is about far more than just your goals and dreams. It asks you to question the beliefs, values, actions, and behaviors to which you're accustomed. It asks you to question whether those things you currently hold close are serving you well for future growth. It is about changing the way you see the world—your world—for future growth. It doesn't matter whether the box is pretty from the outside or forbidding or plain; what matters is that the contents inside the box is intentional, valuable, and actionable for forward growth.

THINKING OUTSIDE THE BOX

> It is not enough to think out of the box. Thinking
> is passive. Get used to acting out of the box.
> —Tim Ferriss

One December, I was on a business trip in Bosnia and Herzegovina. I was there with my colleagues at a holiday party after a long day of engagements. We were having a white-elephant gift exchange—this is where you take turns selecting a wrapped gift from a pile. You can keep your gift, or you can "steal" an already-unwrapped gift from someone else. If you steal a gift, the person from whom you have stolen the gift gets to pick a new gift. When it was my turn, the gift I selected from the pile didn't excite me very much. The person after me, however, selected a beautiful, small, carved wooden box. She wasn't very excited by it and called it "a box of nothing." I wanted it badly but knew that in order for me to get it, someone would have to steal my gift. Thankfully, that happened shortly afterward, and I was able to get the "box of nothing."

When I did, I said to the team, "We will take this box of nothing, and this coming year, we will fill it with something." My goal was to ensure that we continued to add value to the work that we were doing with our partners. I wanted to ensure that the things we set out to accomplish were tangible and amounted to forward movement. I had commented on it without a theory behind it, but when I returned from the trip, the words I'd said continued to run through my mind.

As I looked for a place to put my new box, I realized that I had a number of boxes of different shapes and sizes, including the original silver one that had been my grandmother's. Some were plain; some were beautiful and fancy, but all of them were empty. I wondered why I had received so many boxes as gifts and why I loved them all so much. Then it struck me: our lives without purpose are similar to empty boxes.

This is literally thinking outside of the box. At that moment, I thought of "what's in your box" as a metaphor for designing your life. I realized how such a simple concept could be very powerful. It's all about what you put into it being related to what you get out of it.

We may feel that people are putting us into a box we don't want to be in. We may feel that we are thinking in a box or that we are operating within the constraints of a box. My goal is to get you to consider a physical box as a way to challenge the way you see yourself and your goals, today and in the future. It is about taking control of what a box represents and transforming it into something that helps you go forward in an intentional way.

Even though a box has physical limitations, it is really our thinking that limits us. It isn't the box's physical limits that restricts us or narrows our imaginations; rather, we can use the box in exactly the opposite way. We can put anything in the box that represents a future goal, dream, want, or need. Everything in the box and about the box is focused on getting us to work at our full potential.

While I realized the power of intentionality at the height of my career, I thought how useful it could be if our young adults could grasp this concept earlier on in their lives. It could completely alter the way they approached their lives and belief systems in a constructive way. If you see a box only as a limitation, then you are limited in your thinking. My goal is to tear away that limitation in your thinking and make you believe otherwise.

IS THE BOX ALL THERE IS?

> There is a little bit of magic in every box.
> —Adam Rex

The way we see ourselves is what we become. Our own self-image becomes a self-fulfilling prophecy. The box is a useful tool for allowing us to see ourselves in a way that allows us to become our best selves. We can manifest our future by ensuring the box is never empty.

Self-confidence and self-belief are appealing terms, but in order to be successful, we need to add more to the recipe of success. We need to add determination and passion to follow our goals to the main ingredients. The problem is that most people don't know what their passions are. Many people who find their passions just stumble on them when they least expect it, or they find their passions later in life. They usually don't find them intentionally—at least not in the beginning.

Many people are stuck in a pattern. We limit our own imaginations by underestimating our skills and potential. It is natural to have self-doubt and to call that self-doubt something more positive, such as humility. In a limited way, this is okay. But when self-doubt triumphs over self-belief, it becomes a problem. It makes us wonder if we are capable of meeting our goals. We reconsider our ambitions, which hinders our progress.

The box theory is an approach to work incrementally toward achieving milestones and objectives that are focused on developing your passions. The box makes it easier for you to analyze your growth and learn the aspects of your life's purpose in a more directed way. Simply put, when you identify a goal, you place it in your box. When that goal is achieved, you take the lessons learned from your journey and place them in the box, and put your new goal in your box as well. The method is a way of creating accountability for yourself by keeping your goal contained.

This is where you must take off the blindfold, get real with your values and beliefs, dig deeply into the depths of your heart, and think about moving toward what you enjoy. Finding your stride and using it to advance toward your passion projects requires work. Sometimes, it cannot be achieved without walking many paths. You have to transcend and experience what life has to offer.

We are all meant to shine and achieve different things, but in order to do so, we first need to realize that we have the potential to transcend our self-imposed limitations.

It would be easy to leave the box empty and just enjoy it for its decorative nature. But would that be wise? It would also be easy to escape the responsibility of making the most out of life by not putting forth the effort necessary to overcome the obstacles in front of you. It isn't easy to move out of your comfort zone and try what seems to be impossible. It is much easier to conform to the restrictions imposed upon you by both intrinsic and extrinsic stimuli and pressures, and it takes a lot of courage to rise above them.

If you are too comfortable with the way things are going in your life, personally and professionally, you are no more driving yourself on the on the path to success than you are a passenger in a taxi. Think about it: being comfortable consumes all the enthusiasm you need to excel. You can't be excited about being comfortable. You need enthusiasm to propel you to the next level. Don't confuse being comfortable with being content with where you are.

There can be multiple reasons why you would not want a box in your life to help lead you toward your goals. You may have self-imposed limitations that dominate your thinking. You might not identify with your authentic self. It takes a lot of hard work to succeed, and if, in any way, you intend to avoid the tough slog through this phase of intentionality, there is a good chance that success is beyond your grasp.

Is the Box Half Empty or Half Full?

I don't think out of the box. I think of what I can do with the box.
—Anonymous

At one point or another, you might have been asked if you are the sort of person who see the glass as half empty or half full. Do you remember your response? Do you remember the idea behind the question?

Is there a right or wrong answer to this question? It is all about perspective. Both answers are true. When we look at the psychological perspective alone, there is a lot we can learn from it. The case we are making here, however, focuses on how those psychological theories are put into action.

Just like the glass, your box can be half full or half empty. Your answer hinges on how you see the world. The box theory is not about how full or empty your box is. It is about how you think about the things that you put in your box. Focus on the items in your box that are designed to move your forward.

It is possible that your box will fill up sooner than expected. This means that your box might have a lot of stuff in it, but not all of it is important or useful. The things in your box might just be distractions that take you away from achieving your goals.

Let's discuss the two perspectives projected through the box theory:

The first perspective is designed for the person who is hopeful and optimistic, who sees the glass as half full. These are the individuals who want to continue to pile as much as they can into the glass or, in this case, the box. They measure their level of success based on the fullness of their glasses.

The second perspective is for the people who see things from a more pessimistic or negative worldview. They are stymied by obstacles and are constantly aware of the forces that are working against them. When asked the question, they always answer that the glass is half empty.

I want to challenge you to completely change the paradigm of measuring success in terms of how full or empty your box is. I want you to begin thinking in terms of being intentional about your goals, beliefs, values, and overall journey. I want you to be focused on continual improvement.

There are many ways to invent and reinvent yourself. Many times, we talk about theories and programs that are so abstract that they are hard to implement. My goal with the box theory is to provide you with a simple, logical, and visual way to achieve success throughout your life. Using the box theory, you can transform your thinking, inspire creativity, and align your goals with your beliefs, values, and intentions. The box theory encourages you to be the engineer of your own life, simplifying your vision and opening up a new world of possibilities.

The box is a visual representation of you and your desires, goals, and dreams. It is focused on achieving those things. Now that you know more about your box, ask yourself again if your box is truly empty. If the answer is yes, then ask yourself: "Is that empty box truly serving me well?"

No one's box should truly be empty. Your life is not truly empty. If you think that yours is, you need to take off your blinders, look inside your box, and examine your life. Most of the time, we don't see what is right in front of us. We don't take inventory of what we have accomplished, no matter how small or large the accomplishment. We don't give ourselves credit for climbing the mountain because we don't realize how far we've climbed; we only see ourselves taking one step after another.

After lots of practice, I've trained myself to take inventory, raise my head, set new goals, and dream big dreams—and then work toward them. When I did this systematically, I was astounded of the things I planned and accomplished. It seemed the small things continued to add up to big completing big goals. I didn't realize that the small stuff really adds up in the end to some monumental things. After all, a beach is made up of tiny grains of sand.

I also learned that I had to be intentional to be true to myself and to be happy. I've also learned that we need to redefine what we think of as success. What does it really mean to be successful? If you truly examine this question, you will find things you could never imagine you can achieve or dream of achieving. But you can. This is all your latent potential; you need only to identify it, utilize it, and design your future to your liking.

FILL UP YOUR BOX

> Enough small boxes, thrown into a big empty box fill it full.
> —Carl Sandburg

When you realize there are no limitations to designing your life, and you can fill it up with whatever you desire, that's when you can truly set new boundaries. Those new boundaries establish the guideposts for you to move toward. Those are not limitations but a way to focus on things that matter and to push the things that don't matter outside of the guideposts.

For example, if you are the quarterback of a football team, are you focused on what is outside of the grid, or are you focused on throwing the ball to complete the pass? If you are distracted by the crowd, you won't be able to accomplish your goal. You need to set boundaries for yourself as a way of getting you where you need to go—the end zone—without those boundaries being a limitation on your progress.

Be accountable to yourself. If you are not accountable to yourself, the probability of success goes down significantly. The purpose of accountability is to own your decisions and actions. Learning from your mistakes and moving forward is key.

The first step in self-accountability is identifying your own mission statement. This is a way of setting expectations for yourself. It does not have to be long. In fact, the more concise, the better. It should be a statement of your goals, aligned with your values, interests, strengths, talents, and skills.

Accountability is more than just negative consequences for going astray. There are times when you should reward yourself as a part of accountability too. Rewards are a way of celebrating the little accomplishments along the way. Giving yourself permission to celebrate fuels your motivation. Celebrating does not have to be anything big. It can be as small as treating yourself to ice cream or dinner with a special person or a celebratory dance. As it relates to the box theory, celebrating the small successes along the way is critical to your progress.

When celebrating, keep in mind that not everything in your box is of equal importance. How you categorize these things are a result of how you prioritize your goals. A key part to the box theory is setting micro-goals as well as larger goals. Achieving each of these goals along the way and celebrating those accomplishments will motivate you to strive for the next one.

If you grasp the concept of setting micro-goals, it can change your mind-set forever. When you do not comprehend that micro-goals are a part of your larger goals, it is easy to lose focus. The larger goal is harder to grasp on an everyday, what-am-I-going-to-do-right-now kind of basis. When you lose focus, you lose momentum, and when you lose momentum, you lose confidence in yourself and lose sight that you are capable of achieving your goals. When you lose credibility, you lose respect. When you lose respect, especially self-respect, it's all over. If you don't take yourself seriously, other people won't either.

The box theory uses the concept of micro-goals—setting smaller, achievable, forward-moving goals. It is not just about filling your box with thousands of micro-goals. It's about achieving your dream and—hopefully—leaving behind a meaningful legacy. When you are intentional about the life you are creating, the effect that you want to have on others, and the impact that you want to make, it touches everyone around you. You must understand that your success indirectly impacts your environment and the way you see the world.

Sometimes the goals you set seem unachievable. We all have those days. These types of goals may not be represented as micro-goals, or it might take more tools to achieve them than what you have in your toolbox. These are also various types of goals that can easily derail your motivation and focus. The box theory micro-goal concept is designed to help you move past getting stuck.

WHAT GOES AROUND COMES AROUND

The goal isn't to live forever. It is to create something that will.
—Chuck Palahniuk

Remember that what you put in your box is there because *you* want to focus on moving toward something larger. If you don't spend the time thinking about the larger goals you want to achieve and breaking them down into micro-goals in order to accomplish them, your effort may lack intensity. The accomplishments you achieve and the results you receive are completely based on how intentional you are. The saying "You reap what you sow" is relevant, as it shows that what you get out of something is what you put into it. You can't grow a tree if you don't plant a seed, and you have to plant the right kind of seed if you want a particular kind of tree. The desired outcomes are solely dependent on what you put into the box. As with your life, what you put in is what you get out.

We have talked a lot about putting things into the box, and you might be asking yourself, "What does it mean to put something into the box?" When we create goals for ourselves, we can use different methods to capture those goals.

The box theory is a micro-goal concept used to write each micro-goal down on a *chit*. A chit, according to *Merriam-Webster's Dictionary*, is a small piece of paper with writing on it.[1] In some of the older religions, however, a chit also means "pure consciousness" or "pure thought." It also has in its meaning a comprehension of the true nature of oneself. The box theory uses this to get you to think deeper about your goals by placing only those things you genuinely value in your box. These are not mere pieces of paper: these are representations of meaningful steps toward your ambition.

I want you to visualize your physical box. Choose the color, shape, and size of a box that tickles your fancy. Then, visualize the

---

[1] https://www.merriam-webster.com/dictionary/chit

goals that you want to put in it. If the goals focus on something that will take longer than six months to accomplish, you need to break them down in to micro-goals. Write the goal on the chit, but before you place it in your box, ask yourself, "Are these things aligned with my values, beliefs, and actions?" While this theory sounds simple, it is deceptively so, which we will get into more in later chapters. The box might have initially sounded like a crazy idea, but I hope you now have a clearer understanding of what it is. I've used this idea to completely change my life. It's time you used it to change yours.

As we go through the chapters in this book, I will help you design your box from the ground up. I will help you be thoughtful about the chits you put in your box, based on your personal dreams and goals. In using the box theory in conjunction with the micro-goal concept, you will be able to transform and design your life, based on your dreams. Those dreams can become a reality— one chit, one goal, at a time.

CHAPTER 2

Actions and Behaviors

WHAT ARE YOUR PRIORITIES TODAY? IF YOU WERE TO WRITE DOWN the things you did over the past week, would they be in line with the things you wanted to accomplish? Do you have the right attitude toward your goals?

Action is the process of putting things and ideas into motion. If we are not in motion, we are stagnant. Our actions define us— they tell us a lot about who we are as individuals. Behaviors are a pattern of actions and, in theory, are acquired or learned through conditioning. As a result of this conditioning, we develop patterns that manifest in the way in which we conduct ourselves.

Actions and behaviors go hand in hand. If you intend to change your actions, start off by recognizing how those actions fit into your behavior patterns, and adjust them in a way that best serves your purpose.

Actions and behaviors have the potential to pave the way to success. On the flip side, they also have the potential to sabotage success. It doesn't matter what your goals are; if your actions are not working toward them, you are most likely to fail. This chapter will focus on the actions and behaviors that are required for any person to be successful. Actions and behaviors not only allow us to fulfill our goals but also help us understand whether we are working in concert with our beliefs and values.

DISTINCTIONS: ACTIONS AND BEHAVIORS

Actions are the process of doing or performing something. *Action* refers to a singular occurrence. We often use the word *action* interchangeably with the word *behavior*, but it has a distinct meaning. Actions are intentional and driven by an event-based purpose. An action is a conscious activity that is subject to meaningful activity.

Behavior, on the other hand, is the range of actions and mannerisms made by an individual. Behaviors are not limited to whatever people desire or what they intend to do. Rather, behaviors have a deep relation to the environment, external stimuli, and unconscious internal triggers from previous experiences. Behavior could be considered as the effect an action has on someone other than the actor. The interaction between any two people is largely impacted by the behavior of those two people.

If behavior is the puzzle, actions are the pieces of the puzzle. It is important to understand the difference between the two because knowing the difference will help you align your actions and behaviors in accordance with your goals. While they are two separate entities, distinguished by a thin line, they are equally important for growth and progress.

THE BEHAVIOR CYCLE

> Taking the same path everyday keeps things
> familiar, taking a new path creates growth.

Look at the people around you who are content with whatever life throws their way—you may even be one of them. They think what they say or do doesn't matter because it won't make a difference. They don't try or don't know how to get out of the pattern they are stuck in. Instead of continuing to bang away trying to accomplish their goals, they simply make peace with whatever comes along.

Despite our best efforts to push forward and be different, we sometimes feel like we are playing whack-a-mole or that we're on a carousel ride that never ends. We fall into patterns and ruts and can't seem to break out of them, no matter how hard we try. Does this sound familiar? Have you ever wondered why you are drawn to these same patterns, over and over again? Why do you do what you do?

This pattern is represented in the typical behavior cycle. It begins with an understanding that our conditioned behavior triggers our thoughts and beliefs. These thoughts and beliefs are manifested through our experiences and memories, causing us to act out with feelings and emotions that result in consequences. The key disruptor to these patterns is alignment and intentionality. Without aligning our actions and behaviors toward specific goals, our perspective is cloudy. We are prevented from finding our passion until it is too late.

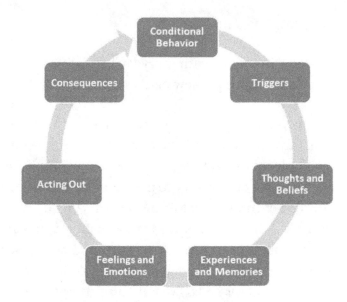

Have you ever wondered why people like Bill Gates and Elon Musk are successful? They are innovative, of course, but it is more than that. They found their drive very early and aligned their actions and behaviors with their intentions. They acted on their thoughts and beliefs.

We cannot act if we don't have the thoughts and experiences to initiate the action. Therefore, it is important to understand that our emotions, feelings, thoughts, and beliefs drive our behaviors. Much of this occurs subconsciously—we may not be aware of it—but there are reasons why we behave the way we do.

CONDITIONED BEHAVIOR

You may have been told that the challenges you encounter on the way to achieving your goals will make you stronger; that dwelling on them won't be any good to you. This is only partially true. There are times when you need to look back and make sure you understand what you went through in order to truly understand where you are going. You need to learn from what happened and adjust accordingly as a result.

This is what the field of psychology calls *classical conditioning*. This is a form of learning, whereby a conditioned stimulus intermixes with an unrelated, unconditioned stimulus. This, in turn, produces a behavioral, or conditioned, response. As an example, it is when a powerful instinctive stimulus, like hunger, is paired with something neutral, like a bell. Thus, whenever you hear a bell, you get hungry.

It is necessary for new stimuli to occur in order for us to learn new behaviors. If the stimulus remains unchanged, so does the behavior. When this occurs over and over, it is called *extinction* because you will either give in or give up—or just be numb to the occurrences. When an individual is in this place, it is possible to reinvigorate the behavioral cycle, but if things get into a yo-yo effect, the bounce back, over time, is slower and slower. We need to continually introduce new stimuli in order to change behavior.

Every now and then on your journey, you will encounter obstacles in your path. Consider these obstacles as nothing more than unconditioned stimuli that you need so you can change your behavior. A typical reaction in these situations is to wish for the obstacles to disappear as rapidly as they appeared. You can wait for them to disappear on their own—but they never will—or you can take them as a new learning experience and work through the various options to overcome them. How you behave is a choice you make, whether you think it is or not.

It may feel as if your behavior just pops out of nowhere. You may wonder why you did what you did. It may seem that your behavior has a mind of its own and takes control of your responses, without your having the ability to control it. Just remember that it is always a choice. It is within your power to recondition your behavioral responses over time. Changing your behavior in the right manner will enable you to look at things differently, thus finding solutions you never thought existed.

We tend to underestimate the effect other people have on our behavior. The types of people with whom we surround ourselves have a great impact on the types of stimuli we encounter. Our parents may have taught us to choose our friends wisely because our parents realized the impact that our social circle has on our behaviors—essentially, that's peer pressure. If we spend more time with people who are not serious about their goals, then our attitudes, most likely, will mimic theirs. We all want to fit in with our peers. This desire to fit in can dramatically shift our perspectives, if we are not careful.

In the bigger picture, your behavior and mind-set are shaped by your environment. This includes the people by whom you are surrounded. You have a choice to be, do, think, and behave differently from them. You may be a product of your environment, but, to some extent, you can choose your environment. Your environment does not have to define who you become.

If you want to achieve something in your life, you will need to continually develop new habits and practices that can improve your behavior. Over time, this strengthens your ability to continually learn, change, and move forward.

TRIGGERS

> If we become aware of what's happening before, we act, behaviour becomes a function of choice rather than a result of an impulse or trigger. You begin to control your world more as opposed to the outside world controlling you.
>
> —Marshall Goldsmith

When behavior takes a dive, something typically has triggered that downward spiral. When we talk about *triggers*, we often are talking about childhood behavior. But it is equally as relevant in adult be-havior. A trigger is nothing more than a thought or a situation—an individual stimulus—that results in an action that leads to undesir-able behavior choices. Our environment, background, social circle, and family life, as well as many other things, are commonly the things that shape what triggers our behaviors.

The challenge that we adults face is that, in many cases, we don't know what triggers our own behaviors. We have no idea where to start to find the root cause, and even if we know, the roots can be so deep that we don't want to deal with them. But if we dig down, we can find a workable solution.

The first step is to find the reason for the negative behavior. Find out what triggers the response. Doing this is finding out what makes you *you*. Only you know how you're feeling and thinking. You are the best—possibly, the only—person to talk to in order to find the missing puzzle piece.

THOUGHTS AND BELIEFS

Your mind is an amazing computer within itself. It is the best tool you have available to you, and it goes with you wherever you go. Even with modern technology, we have not been able to create a machine that works anywhere close to the human mind. Our minds allow us to synthesize so much information. Our thoughts allow us to create our lives, positively and negatively. It is important to understand that our thinking does not solely create our circum-stances. It is our thinking, tied to our emotions, that create our circumstances.

You can think about a lot of things, but those thoughts only manifest into actions when strong emotions and feelings are associ-ated with them. Our thoughts, at first, are just a conscious nudging.

Then, if they are strong enough, we put them into action, and with enough action, they become a part of our subconscious.

The subconscious mind is the keeper of our emotions and memory. The two form a pact that sets things in motion, thus creating an energy that swirls around us. When an emotion is strongly attached to a thought, its ability to move forward is intense. When a thought has a weak emotion or no feeling at all attached to it, there is no energy and no forward movement.

The best example of this is when you concentrate on your imperfections. This focus sets in motion so much that affects the way you see yourself and how others see you. By shifting your thoughts and emotions toward the positive, it can shift the energy all around you as well.

Beliefs are nothing more than collections of thought patterns. You can have many different thoughts going through your mind at a given time. Those that repeat themselves and the ones that you accept as true become your beliefs. Your decision can move thoughts into beliefs and into reality. You have the power to choose which thoughts to make real and which ones to leave as mere flights of fancy. Your thoughts and beliefs are manifested into your actions and behaviors. They are the key to changing your behavior.

EXPERIENCES AND MEMORIES

> Karma, memory, and desire are just the software of the soul. It's conditioning that the soul undergoes in order to create experience. And it's a cycle. In most people, the cycle is a conditioned response. They do the same things over and over again.
>
> —Deepak Chopra

Experiences and memories are two sides of the same coin. You can't have one without the other. What is it about our experiences that contributes to our memories? Why do some experiences make a longer-lasting impression than others? How can two people share the same experience, but each remembers different things about that experience? Experiences are the foundation of memory. While the experience is short-lived, the memory—the take-away—can last forever.

Nobel Prize winner and behavioral economics founder Daniel Kahneman explains that we have "two selves." These are the "remembering-self" and the "experiencing-self." The experiencing-self exists in the present moment. The remembering-self looks back on the experience. When we experience something, we keep the memory of that experience. Depending on the perspective from which we view the experience, our memories will be different. Our memories will affect the decisions and actions we take as a result of this experience. The job of the remembering-self is in the relationship between the two.

In reality, we choose our memories but not necessarily our experiences. This is a key point and one of the main reasons I chose to title my first book, *Moments of Choice*. Life is a succession of moments that we experience. When I wrote *Moments of Choice*, it was my remembering-self that kept those memories nicely tucked away. The remembering-self is critical when we make decisions based on the experiences we remember.

FEELINGS AND EMOTIONS

While we may use the words *emotions* and *feelings* interchangeably, they are distinctly different. Emotions are a physical response; feelings are more of a mental action. Your feelings are stirred up by emotions that get ignited by thoughts and experiences. Just as your memories of an experience can last a lifetime, so can your feelings. Emotions are short-lived, but feelings can endure. Feelings are a collage made of your memories. They are a patchwork quilt made from your thoughts, taken from images and experiences that are subconsciously linked to emotions. This can be a vicious cycle that can spin out of control.

Even though emotions are temporary, the feelings they evoke may continue to increase over time. Feelings are shaped by a person's temperament and experiences. They vary greatly from person to person and in each situation.

Your emotions and feelings play a powerful role in how you engage with and experience the things around you. They are the driving force behind many behaviors, both positive and negative. It is possible to harbor unconscious, fear-based perceptions that affect your decisions and your life in general, even though you don't feel fearful at the moment.

We tend to subconsciously hold on to these outdated tendencies that pop up at the most inconvenient times. Becoming aware of deep-seated feelings and emotions is the best method for heading off any issues that are displayed outwardly.

ACTING OUT

Most people don't really think about their emotions and feelings before they act, even though their emotions and feelings are the root cause of their actions. Becoming more aware of your emotions and feelings gives you the ability to be deliberate in your actions and to navigate the roads of your life in a purposeful way. You can do this only when you are in control of your responses. This can make the difference between living life in complete chaos, letting life happen on its own, or finding the right amount of healthy tension to create alignment.

This is not to suggest that finding alignment means that everything is roses and chocolates. Healthy tension does mean that you can provide what is necessary to align your actions and behaviors with your beliefs and values and therefore control the outcomes.

Learning how to navigate and use alignment to your benefit requires you to straddle your memories, experiences, feelings, and emotions to create synergy, instead of just energy. Unless you want to live life like a Tasmanian devil, you must strive for control, you must be laser sharp and intentional in changing your thinking and behavior. Be aware; be in the moment. Don't let things from your past dominate your future or prevent you from accomplishing your goals.

If we pause and take a breath in between our emotions, feelings, and actions, we will realize that the power to change our behavior resides within us. We have the ability to learn to manage this trio. Our emotions don't have the power to hijack our feelings—if we don't allow them to do so. We don't have to give them permission to wreak havoc on our behavior, although it will take practice to hone this technique.

You must practice the ability to slow down and give yourself the moment you need to allow your thoughts and your response mechanism to assemble. Not doing this prior to taking action may result in your using a sledgehammer when all you needed was a screwdriver.

CONSEQUENCES

Consequences are the outcomes of action. They are some of the most important elements in the behavior cycle. Consequences can be positive or negative, but they serve as fuel to our behaviors to start the cycle all over again.

Our goal should be to understand the impact of our behaviors, which means also understanding the consequences of our behaviors. We need to be cautious not to perpetuate negative behavior. We must disrupt negative behavior by dealing with the consequence by not taking the action that resulted in the negative consequence in the first place.

There are two types of consequences: natural and logical. Logical consequences are those that require a level of intervention. Natural consequences are those that follow a choice or behavior naturally. For example, if you got caught speeding, a logical consequence would be that you would get a ticket and have to pay a fine. That would then result in your being more cautious and not speeding. If you jumped into a cold shower, a natural consequence would be that you would jump right back out or otherwise physically react to the cold water. The reaction is not man-made.

People ultimately do what they do because of the consequences they experience as a result of their behaviors. How consequences are handled can be an effective tool to strengthen desired behaviors and weaken undesired ones.

Let's briefly examine the impact of consequences in the workplace. Bad behaviors in the workplace can result in a decrease in productivity. They can impact employee engagement and may cost the company business.

Whether you are dealing with minor problems or significant issues, how you deal with the situation is key. Consequences are a normal result of behavior. You must be accountable for your actions and be willing to deal with the consequences of your actions. If you can't bear the consequences, then don't take the actions. Take a stand, here and now, and break the vicious cycle of negative behavior. Don't allow it to continue. If you control your actions, you will find that the consequences will match the action. Ideally, the consequences will be rewarding.

Box Thoughts

1. Are your actions and behaviors aligned with your goals?
2. What new habits will you create to move toward your goals?
3. How can you discard old behaviors to make room for new ones?

CHAPTER 3

Promises

People with good intentions make promises.
People with good character keep them.
—unknown

DO YOU MAKE PROMISES AND THEN FIND YOURSELF MAKING RA-
tionalizations for why you didn't keep them? Or are you one of
those people who avoids making promises at all costs? How do you
feel when someone breaks a promise to you?

I have found that many people seem to have no problem breaking promises. They forget about them as soon as they make them,
or they don't take their promises seriously. Your promises set up
expectations that you will do what you say you will do. Keeping
your promise builds a sense of trust and comfort in other people.
They know that when you say you will do something, you will stick
to your word.

You may have individuals in your inner circle who have never failed to come through for you. You also may have those around you who never seem to come through at all. You know who is reliable and who isn't. The big question is, who do you want to be?

The dictionary definition of a promise is a declaration, whether written or verbal. A promise is an assurance or vow that a certain act is agreed upon and will happen. We know the basic definition, but do we truly understand the meaning and context that a promise takes in the grand scheme of things?

We make promises all the time. Sometimes, we don't even realize that we have made a promise. It could be something small, like promising to attend a party or delivering a project on time. The more we are known to keep our promises, the more trusted we are and the more confidence others will have in our abilities. Making and breaking promises can become a habit, just like any other type of behavior. Like anything, creating a habit of making promises and keeping them takes practice, patience, and honesty.

Think about the promises, big and small, that you've made in the last few days. To whom did you make promises? Why did you make them? Did you make any promises to yourself? Now, ask the most important question: did you keep your promises to yourself, or did you keep only the ones to others?

SELF-PROMISES

While you might be the kind of person who wouldn't even consider breaking a promise to another person, you may not have any trouble breaking a promise to yourself. We often habitually betray ourselves because we don't see this as a breach of trust or commitment. We don't take promises to ourselves seriously. In fact, we convince ourselves that this is acceptable behavior and it doesn't really matter.

We value commitments to others more than commitments to

ourselves. When we do this over and over, it gets easier, and we end up doing it subconsciously. This type of behavior makes it significantly difficult to make meaningful and lasting change.

The next time you make a promise to anyone, think about making one to yourself. Apply the same level of energy to keep your promise to yourself that you would for others. This will empower you in ways you could not imagine.

Making promises to yourself increases your strength, confidence, and self-esteem, and it makes you realize your true self-worth. Of course, making promises to yourself will be of no good unless you keep them. You have to start by making them; then keep them. Value yourself as much as you value others, and see where it takes you.

To begin taking yourself more seriously, you must become more aware of the commitments you make. You'll have to practice self-discipline, and remember that trust is built through a series of experiences. When your behavior is consistent, you will get consistent results. You need to believe that breaking a small promise is just as important as breaking a large one. A promise is a promise, no matter the size.

PROMISE PACT

If you are going to develop the habit of making self-promises, start with developing a promise pact. A promise pact is a contract with yourself. Write down this promise pact in an agreement that clearly reflects what you want; then put this agreement in your box. The more details it contains about what you want to do or stop doing and the results you expect, the better it will be.

Take stock of what it will take to complete this pact. Think about what the value will be to you for keeping this promise. Act as if your life depends on keeping this contract—because it does. Be clear about the pact and its importance to you.

You might be thinking, *I have no time to do this and no idea how to develop a contract.* Don't overcomplicate things. It doesn't have to be a legally sound or lengthy document. Make it simple. Just break it down into micro-goals and put each one on a chit to make your promises. Put each chit in your box. Your box serves as a reminder of what you want to get out of life, and this includes the promises you make. Using promises to accelerate growth is a sure way to increase your likelihood of success.

Following are a few ways you can work on making and keeping promises as a habit.

A PROMISE A DAY

Starting off small with a promise a day is a way to slowly improve on keeping your promises. This is one of the most powerful tools available to you. Each one takes you closer to accomplishing your goal, especially if they are promises that you make to yourself.

If they are promises you make to others, they build your credibility. Building your credibility also can help build your self-esteem and confidence.

Start with something small and easy to accomplish. Tell yourself you are going to make your bed every morning, or you are going to call your friend today. Starting with small, achievable promises with easy outcomes will lessen the weight of the promise altogether. You can't predict the outcome of what the promise will do for you, but you can predict how it will make you feel. When you decide on the promise you will make today, think about how you will feel once it is completed. Think about that sense of satisfaction and of a job well done.

It is very rewarding to change behavior. With promises, it is even more than that; it is a test of our integrity. Integrity is to honor one's word. If we find ourselves faltering, we must own up to it. We must recommit to ourselves or others and then move on. Keeping our promises is the key to achieving the life we dream of. Our promises should empower us to grow, reach, and dream big.

SET LOGICAL AND ACHIEVABLE PROMISES

When you begin to make and fulfill your promises, pay special attention to whether you have the capability to deliver on what you have promised. You may need to do a significant amount of work before the promise can be fulfilled. Don't promise more than you can deliver. This includes the promises you make to others as well as the promises you make to yourself.

If you know what you are promising is destined to fail, rethink your strategy. If you don't, then your thinking is not realistic. You are sabotaging your own efforts.

Don't overcommit yourself. Overcommitting is a common problem because we don't want to say no or to let people down. Regardless of how you analyze this, overcommitting is just as bad as not having the capability to deliver on the promise. Sometimes, the kindest and best thing to do is to say no in the first place. Both overcommitment and incapability will cause you to break your promise or deliver on it very poorly.

If you promise someone world peace, there is no way you could deliver on that promise. Baking cupcakes for a bake sale sounds a whole lot more achievable, but not if you are scheduled day and night before the deadline and don't have the ingredients on hand. We've all had those frantic moments of exhaustion, where our promises have clashed with our overall schedule, and we can't figure out how to cram thirty hours of effort into a twenty-four-hour day.

The key is to be realistic about what you can do by knowing your capabilities and strengths. Take your time before making the promise. Don't rush to failure. If you are the one who tends to mismanage your time, maybe the first promise you should make to yourself is to get better at time management—or to simply learn to say no.

BE COMMITTED

> Commitment is what transforms a promise into reality. It is the words that speak boldly of your intentions. And the actions which speak louder than the words. It is making the time when there is none. Coming through time after time after time, year after year after year. Commitment is the stuff character is made of; the power to change the face of things. It is the daily triumph of integrity over skepticism.
>
> —Abraham Lincoln

What does the word *commitment* suggest to you? It usually evokes a strong sense of intention and focus. It is accompanied by a statement of purpose or a plan of action. We often think it has the same meaning for all of us, which isn't the case. People who know the true meaning of commitment value the power that a true commitment can wield.

As with our promises, we find it easier to commit to others than to ourselves. Some find it a struggle to commit to anything at all. There are so many ways in which people commit. Some of them are personal and some more professionally focused. We usually only focus on what we are committed to. We forget about an equally important part: how we originally committed to this goal.

As with everything else you do, the main thing about commitments is the effort you put into the them. How you do or do not commit becomes a part of the script of your life. It is critical that you pay close attention to how you engage in commitments. The work that you put into preparing for what you have committed to essentially dictates your level of success.

There are three main commitment areas that you should consider:

1. relationships and who you spend your time with
2. places where you spend your time
3. what you do with your time

The area that influences your decisions the most will be the area that has the strongest pull on your feelings. If you are conscious about the area in which you make commitments and ensure that they are aligned with your interests and passions, you will be more likely to be successful in delivering on that promise.

There will be times when you have made a commitment but feel it isn't worth the price you will pay to fulfill that commitment. Call it for what it is. You may be making excuses for why you can't keep the commitment, or maybe you aren't capable of fulfilling it.

Fulfilling any commitment requires discipline and, at times, getting out of your comfort zone. This is truly where the rubber meets the road. Face whatever fear or challenge is in front of you. Keep your reputation intact and your integrity in mind as you move forward. As much as you may not want to fulfill your commitment, what are the consequences for not doing so?

You may realize that things are not going as planned—perhaps you've had a shift in priorities, or your resolve is on a slippery slope. Then you will need to reevaluate and reinforce what you have committed to. If it isn't working, ask yourself: "Why isn't it working like it is supposed to? Am I giving it all I have? Have I set unrealistic expectations?"

It's necessary to work to identify the specific reasons why what you are doing is not working. Commitments can define and shape your behavior. They can reinforce old behaviors just as well as they can transform behaviors. The commitments you make and keep must be consistent with your ethos, values, and actions. Your commitments enable, constrain, and provide continuity over time. They make you who you are. They are what moves you from being good to being great.

TELL THE WHOLE TRUTH

You likely have heard the standard oath given in a courtroom. Witnesses aren't just asked to tell the truth; they are asked to swear to tell "the truth, the whole truth, and nothing but the truth." I wanted to focus on this because telling the *whole truth* is one of my pet peeves. People exaggerate, stretch, or omit things in order to sway their version of the truth.

What never ceases to amaze me is that when people make promises and then falter on them, they feel like they can alter the truth to justify their behavior. This happens way too often in today's environment.

There used to be a time in which our word was significant, and we took immense pride in maintaining our reputation for good character. There also was a time when we instilled integrity in our children at a very early age. We were taught that character was an integral part of success. I remember being told that if I lied, I would be banished to the depths of hell—talk about instilling fear! As a young child, I had no idea what hell was, but I knew it was bad, and I knew I didn't want to go there.

The point was not about the place itself but about reinforcing the importance of telling the truth. I knew that telling my parents the truth was paramount, and the consequences for failing to do so were severe.

Do you know that there are two kinds of lies—lies of commission and lies of omission? When people tell you things that simply are not true, those are lies of commission. Some people like to stretch or twist the truth into something that does not resemble what actually happened or is a completely distorted version of what happened. You don't want to put yourself in this situation. People who do this usually lack consistency in their stories and lack credibility over time. While lying may not have been their intention as they set out telling their stories, they decided to embellish their versions for a variety of reasons. Maybe it made them feel important or made them look better. Maybe it just sounded better. Whatever the reason, you need to ensure that when you make promises, you tell the truth as it occurred, even if it is not a pretty truth.

A lie of omission is where you intentionally omit an important detail from a statement. This missing detail changes the meaning of what you are saying. You don't want to do this either; it can be just as deceitful as lying outright.

Your word is symbolic of your honor and credibility. Every time you make a promise, you are putting your reputation on the line. If you lie as a foundation for why you were not able to fulfill your commitment or as a part of fulfilling your commitment, what does it say about you? You must live up to your word. Take pride in the standards that you set for yourself. Realize that you will be taken at face value. If you have a reputation for truthfulness, you will be believed. If you have a reputation for falsehoods, you will not be believed, even when you are telling the truth. You may think you are fooling the world, but you are only fooling yourself. Your word should be your bond. When all is said and done, a promise is a promise.

Box Thoughts
1. What promise can you make to yourself and keep it?
2. Are there ways you could develop the habit of keeping promises that you make, regardless of how small?
3. What promises do you want to put in your box?

CHAPTER 4

Intention

Intentions compressed into words
enfold magical power.
—Deepak Chopra

INTENTIONS ARE YOUR GUIDING PRINCIPLES FOR HOW YOU WANT to be, live, and show up in the world. Intentions are not to be confused with goals. They aren't something to which you attach an evaluation. Intentions are what you want to align with. They are aims, purposes, or attitudes that you want to commit to. Intentions evoke feelings and create purpose. Intentions are heart-driven. Nothing happens without intention; everything hangs on it. Your goals are created around your intentions and are made possible because of your intentions, but they are not the same as your intentions.

THE CONCEPT OF INTENTIONS

Intentions are best explained through Buddhist teachings. Buddhism highlights intentions as one of the crucial components in the eightfold path. Your intentions should be closely tied to your personal thoughts, values, and perspective on life.

Wise intentions keep us going in the right direction and following the right path. Consider this: when you are hiking in the woods, your intention is to follow the path to get you to your campsite. If the path ends, you still need to get to your campsite. You realize that the sun should always remain on your right in order to get to the correct location, so you continue to walk through the woods, keeping the sun on your right side. In this case, the sun is like your intention, as it guides you in the right direction. Wise intention is what keeps us on the right path.

How do you know if the intentions that you are putting in your box are wise ones?

It is the cornerstone of focused and wise effort. In order to ensure that your efforts are wise and not wasted, you must continually evaluate and reevaluate your actions. Only choose the actions that keep you as close to your path as possible. Check to see if you are being true to yourself; this will ensure that your intentions are wholesome and correct.

Setting your intentions is like drawing a map of where you want to go. It becomes the guiding force of your higher consciousness. Without this metaphorical road map, you are just driving aimlessly, hoping you get where you want to be.

Buddhist teaching says that goal-making is something that takes the focus away from being in the present. By definition, goals are in the future. Focusing on goals alone keep you forward-looking. There is nothing wrong with looking ahead, but if you focus solely on the future and not the present, you can't see where you are. This brings about anxiety and potential failure.

Focusing on the present can allow you to focus on attainment of a higher state. This helps you understand your core values and what you stand for. Intentions are about being in the present moment and living according to your values. They are about using your power to focus and be deliberate in your actions. This will help you reach your goals. Intentions should reflect what is more important to you. They align with what you want in life, your inner values, and your belief in what is possible. When your intention follows this path, then you are heading in the right direction, and achievement of your goals will be at the end of the road.

Meditation and other methods of reflection to focus on your intention increases the likelihood of forward movement. Creating a habit of intentionality requires focus and daily practice. It isn't something that just occurs; it must be deliberate. Your intentions need to focus within the framework of thinking, being, and doing.

Intention is focused on keeping you in perpetual motion. As soon as you get stuck in any one place, your forward momentum stops. Your actions and intentions get out of alignment. Think of the earth traveling around the sun. If it were to suddenly stop, part of the earth would remain in darkness, the tides would be affected, and the entire planet would be out of alignment with the solar system. This is the same premise.

WASTED INTENTIONS

Have you ever felt like you were running on ice—like all your concerted effort, focus, and everything you have been doing is not getting you anywhere? If you feel this way, it is likely because your intentions are set in the wrong direction. Just like driving along the wrong highway won't get you to your destination, no matter how many hours you spend behind the wheel, working with the wrong intentional mind-set won't help you achieve your goals.

In many cases, you won't realize this is what you have been doing until you are on the wrong side of things. Even if you have the best of intentions—you mean well; you thought you were doing the right things—you can lose your way and get derailed. You may have had all the right intentions starting out, but you ended up on the wrong path. This is a real problem for many of us. There are a lot of distractions along the way. We get busy and forget to do things with intention and purpose. We go about our daily routines, doing things the same way, day in and day out, because that's the way we've always done them.

Think about what you do every day. Do you plan the next day in the evening, or do you plan the week on Monday morning? When you go about your day, are you deliberately following the plan that you put in place? If not, why not?

How many times have you thought about starting and sticking with an exercise program or going back to school—and then didn't follow through? Do you check your phone in the morning before you have even brushed your teeth? Do you check your email before you have attempted to do other necessary things?

It isn't a matter of whether what you are doing is right or wrong. There is no absolute right or wrong when considering your activities, unless it is clearly something that breaks the law. The question is why you are doing what you are doing. Is what you are doing contributing to your specific aim or end goal? Are you spending your time working on someone else's must-do list? Focusing on the intentions of others drains the energy you need to focus on your own intentions. If you're not careful, your mental capacity and energy will waste away on whatever is loud enough to grab your attention and not what is on the quieter path toward your destination.

Intention is a state of mind that is gradually developed with continued practice. Like any other thing, the longer you practice on being intentional, the more it becomes a habit in the way you go about your day. You will begin to provide the space for other things to emerge that were previously blocked by wasted intentions. You may not realize how much of your subconscious drives your actions.

Be sure that your subconscious and conscious minds are fully aligned. Your conscious mind has to be completely engaged in what you are doing. When your subconscious mind is driving the conscious, it often gets away from you with negative thoughts. Your subconscious can hijack your intention and land you back in the wasteland. That pesky little subconscious gremlin begins playing all our negative thoughts on a loop: "I'm not good enough"; "I can't do this"; "I don't deserve this." If you let the gremlin stay in control, running rampant, you will never reach your goals. This is the definition of wasted intentions.

WHAT IS YOUR INTENT?

In order to ensure that your intent isn't wasted, be sure that you are fully aware of what your intent is. You need to be constantly mindful of your true intent in order to manifest your intent. Whether you are at a business meeting or social event or are visiting a sick friend, ask yourself, "What is my true intent?" Regardless of whether you are at an event to grow your social circle, to increase business, or simply to have a good time, it's important to know why you are there in the first place.

Sometimes we are not certain of what our intentions truly are. Our belief systems might try to argue with our intentions when our actions contradict them. This happens when our intentions are confused. Assessing the *why* behind everything you do will help you focus on whether your intent is aligned with your actions, and vice versa.

BAD INFLUENCES

Oftentimes, our feelings and emotions influence our intentions. This isn't always a bad thing, but it can get tricky when we are going through a difficult phase in our lives. In these times, clarity is the only thing that can save us. Evaluating and examining our intentions can be quite an eye-opener. If we sincerely step back and take a look at what we are doing, we can surprise ourselves.

Consider what your intention is behind setting a particular goal. It may be to achieve something greater and work for a higher purpose, or it could be to accomplish something others want you to do. If you are doing the latter, is this simply to make someone else happy, or is it to work your way up the ladder and achieve the promotion you have dreamed of? Think about what purpose it serves. If it doesn't serve your purpose, the chances of achieving your goals are minimal.

It isn't always that simple. Sometimes, fear and anger, combined with frustration and resentment, can fuel our intentions. This is rarely productive. This happens generally when we are confident that we can restrict someone from carrying out an action.

Discuss your intentions with the people around you. Be very sure of what you truly want. Your intentions are like the salt in a recipe. It isn't the main ingredient, but it can make your food taste great or too salty, depending on how focused you are on creating an amazing meal.

KARMA

Karma is real. What goes around really does come around. We hope that our good actions aren't in vain, and they aren't. Likewise, our negative actions will have negative repercussions. Life will return good things to us if we do good things; life will return bad things to us if we do bad things.

Karma is independent of what we want for ourselves. It is more reliant on our actions and what we do. It is an independent analysis of how we have behaved, based on our intentions.

If you are looking for ways to escape karma, you are fighting against the impossible. You are fighting against the very fabric of the universe and the all-encompassing energy of the planet. Your intentions matter. Even if your actions are perceived as positive by the outside world, if the action was driven by a negative intention, you will reap what you have sown.

For example, you may do something wonderfully charitable. Perhaps you give a lot of money to a good cause, or you spend a day building a house with Habitat for Humanity. These are good things, and you may receive a lot of praise for them. But if your intention was not to ensure that the charity had enough money to do its good works but rather to make sure that you were seen as a good person and receive praise, was your intention a good one? If you only went to Habitat for Humanity because the guy or gal you had your eye on was there and you wanted to impress him or her, and you hated every minute of it, was your intention pure? Karma will not treat you based on how the world perceives your actions. Karma will treat you based on your intentions.

In order to be effective, your intentions must be pure. Purity of mind and intention helps you acquire a peace of mind. When your mind is peaceful, you can accept whatever fortune comes your way. Your intentions need constant checks and balances to ensure that they are pure in every moment and situation. It is easy to stray from the path. Pure intentions construct a pathway for you to achieve your goals.

It's about setting the right tone. You won't have only a single goal throughout your life. Your goals and ambitions will change as you grow and mature and as you reach certain milestones. You constantly will add and remove chits from your box. If you develop a habit of making sure that your intentions are pure, you also will develop a habit of achieving your goals.

It is wise to calm your enthusiastic mind and become more focused on your intentions. It can't hurt to spare a minute before making a phone call or walking into a meeting room to take a mental check and reassure yourself that your approach and plan of action are on the right track.

Gradually, we learn to add kindness and compassion to our intentions. We all come from different backgrounds. Our actions and intentions are necessarily influenced by our pasts. When our intentions are pure, we wash out the negativity and become more compassionate and understanding. The secret to making appropriate actions is pure intentions. Therefore, it is necessary to examine our intentions before carrying out any actions.

SETTING THE INTENTION CORRECTLY

Let's talk about a few steps you can take to correctly set your intentions. It isn't necessarily the only method, but this three-step process has worked for me, and it will surely work for you, if you allow it to do so.

1. Start with making true, desired intentions.

Setting intentions is the starting point. No matter what your goals are, the first thing you need to begin the journey to your goals is the intention. Intention-setting allows you to serve a greater purpose, as it helps you identify what you truly want.

Real desire is the strongest force in helping you to achieve your goals. Although intentions are independent of outcome, true desire maximizes the chances of a positive result. Whenever you set a goal, ask yourself if it is something you truly want. Otherwise, the effort will be wasted. Even if you manage to be successful in achieving your goal, it will not give you happiness.

The key here is to ask yourself why. Before you place any goal in your box, ask yourself why you are doing it. Let your heart take command and guide you toward accomplishing your target. When you involve your soul in achieving a specific goal, it will resonate in your whole body, and you will know it is right.

It is not worth having the stress and going through the hardship in pursuit of something you do not truly want. As Oprah Winfrey put it:

> Before you agree to do anything that might add even the smallest amount of stress to your life, ask yourself: What is my truest intention? Give yourself time to let a yes resound within you. When it's right, I guarantee that your entire body will feel it.

2. Believe—The outcome is not important.

It is a lot easier to say you are going to let go than to let go of your attachments. But just because something is difficult doesn't mean you should avoid it. Letting go of your negative attachments will keep you inspired. It helps you stay joyful, even while you are on the journey of accomplishing your goals.

Having negativity around us while we are pursuing our goals prevents us from progressing. It is vital for us to work on our negative emotions in order to lead a better life. We need a proper plan of action, but a plan of action, in and of itself, is not enough. Behind positive intentions, there needs to be positive energy to ensure that we see our goals through.

There is always the possibility that things will happen in a way that is contrary to your hopes. Always be open to every aspect of reality, including the ones you'd rather not have happen. You place your trust in the universe when you force a positive intention into your belief system. This does not mean that you stop thinking about your goals or stop being optimistic about achieving them. It means you take new considerations and events into account as they occur and accept whatever the outcome is. Your belief in the process is what is important, not the individual outcomes along the way.

3. Intentions are only a prerequisite to your plan of action.

It is impossible to stand any chance of achieving your goals if the actions are not there. It's like the intentions are a canvas on which you paint with your actions. Your inner beliefs have to come in line with your physical actions. Your physical actions are what make your goals real.

If you are looking for quick results or instant gratification, you most likely will be disappointed. Intentions are not a magic wand. Intentions are dependent on actions. You need to act accordingly, not letting negative emotions, like fear, blow you off course and prevent you from working toward your goals. Working on your mind-set is critical. Otherwise, there will come a point when things get difficult, and you might consider giving up on your goals.

Don't let a lack of outside support or accountability factor into your achievement. They should have nothing to do with your own personal intention or actions. Your intentions lead to your actions. Don't let other people affect that.

LIGHT FROM WITHIN

A great example of someone whose intention seemed to be consistent and pure is Mother Teresa. Mother Teresa's life was phenomenal because she made it so. None of it happened overnight, and there was a lot of hard work and dedication behind it. What really made her triumph, however, was the purity of her intention and her passion for others.

She is a great example for us to understand the importance of intention. She had a clear vision from a very early age. She knew she wanted to help humanity and had no doubts about it. She understood as a young adult that her intentions had to be pure, and she never modified them. This does not mean that she did not lose her way at times or that everything was easy. Regardless of the challenging times, however, she stayed on course with the best of intentions.

Her intention was simple: she wanted to help humanity. As time passed, her concerns about the people around her only increased. She added fighting poverty as a goal. She provided for the needy. She may not have had an action plan when she started out, but she had a pure intent. Because she had clarity, developing an action plan was not difficult for her.

I can only assume that her box was her holy book. While it may not have been apparent to us, it is likely that she had many goals in her box. But before she had those specific goals, she had pure, honest intentions. If it weren't for that clarity in her vision and the priority of her intentions, she wouldn't have received the universally beloved title of *Mother*. This is what pure intentions do. They open you up to broader prospects, thereby enabling you to realize other important things in life. They allow you to become part of something greater than yourself, even beyond your own expectations.

I am not asking you to be like Mother Teresa, but I am asking you to consider what is deep within. Your intentions are critically essential for setting your goals and achieving them. Your entire box and journey are dependent on the intention. Intention is what adds value to the contents of your box. No matter what your goals are and how committed you are in fulfilling them, the absence of intention is destined to push you astray. Mother Teresa did not achieve what she did without intention, and none of the people like her did either. You too have the potential to be great in your own right. Begin by tuning your intentions to greatness and perfection. It is something you can control.

Box Thoughts

1. What are your intentions?
2. Why are you doing what you do?
3. Are your intentions aligned with your goals?

CHAPTER 5

Beliefs and Values

YOUR BELIEFS AND VALUES ARE SOME OF THE CORE COMPONENTS that you will address as you place items inside your box. Let's start by looking at what beliefs and values are and how they are different from one another.

> Your beliefs become your thoughts, your thoughts become your words, your words become your actions, your actions become your habits, your habits become your values, your values become your destiny.
> —Gandhi

WHAT ARE BELIEFS AND VALUES?

Beliefs are certain assumptions you make about the truth of the world. It's easiest to understand these in terms of religious beliefs.

You may believe in the divinity of Jesus Christ, or you may believe in the Hindu gods, or you may believe in any of the other gods in the world's religions. Your belief may or may not be a rational one. In fact, belief often defies logic. It is an unquestionable reality for you, and it is what you base your understanding of the world around.

Not all beliefs are as large as religion. You may believe that yellow is everyone's' favorite color, after all it has to be because it is a pleasing, happy color. You may believe in Santa Claus or the Tooth Fairy. You may believe in ghosts or the existence of Bigfoot.

Values, on the other hand, are a measure of what you hold important. They may stem from your beliefs. Often, your religion and its teachings will inform what your values are, but they are not the same thing. Your values are what you hold dear.

Values are things like honesty, loyalty, kindness, courage, intelligence, ability, politeness, or strength. You may rank these things differently, or you may or may not value them. Whether they are values that influence what you put in your box is up to you.

WHICH BELIEFS AND VALUES SHOULD YOU CONSIDER?

Which beliefs and values influence your decisions is a very personal decision and is dependent on your past experiences. Look deep inside yourself, and see if you can figure this out. Make a list of your beliefs and values. This will be useful when you are defining your goals.

Most of the time, we do not realize how our beliefs and values can positively or negatively impact our journeys. Reassessing your beliefs and values from time to time is a necessity.

You must ask yourself, "What are my basic beliefs?" Are you a religious or spiritual person? Is there an organization whose tenets align with your own beliefs? Are your beliefs consistent with your actions and behavior? Do you know which of your beliefs and values are holding you back? Do you know which ones are propelling you forward? Are those beliefs aligned with everything inside your box, or do you need to modify it to suit your own needs?

Sometimes, we find it hard to put these things into words. I have compiled a list of beliefs and values for you to consider when assessing your own. Take a look at the following chart.

Acceptance	Depth	Harmony	Peace
Accomplishment	Determination	Helpfulness	Perceptiveness
Achievement	Devoutness	Holiness	Perfection
Adventure	Dignity	Honesty	Persistence
Affection	Diligence	Honor	Philanthropy
Affluence	Discipline	Humility	Playfulness
Aggressiveness	Discretion	Humor	Poise
Agility	Dominance	Hygiene	Popularity
Alertness	Drive	Ingenuity	Power
Altruism	Eagerness	Inquisitiveness	Practicality
Ambition	Economy	Integrity	Proactivity
Appreciation	Effectiveness	Intelligence	Professionalism
Approachability	Efficiency	Intensity	Punctuality
Balance	Encouragement	Judiciousness	Reliability
Beauty	Endurance	Justice	Religiousness
Bliss	Enthusiasm	Kindness	Resourcefulness
Bravery	Expertise	Leadership	Self-control
Candor	Exuberance	Liberty	Selflessness
Capability	Fairness	Logic	Serenity
Charity	Faith	Looking good	Sexuality
Chastity	Family	Love	Spirituality
Cheerfulness	Ferocity	Loyalty	Spunk
Cleanliness	Fidelity	Majesty	Temperance
Commitment	Financial Independence	Mastery	Thankfulness
Compassion	Fitness	Maturity	Thoroughness
Composure	Fortitude	Mindfulness	Thoughtfulness
Confidence	Freedom	Mysteriousness	Tranquility
Conviction	Frugality	Nerve	Uniqueness
Correctness	Generosity	Obedience	Variety
Courtesy	Gentility	Open-mindedness	Warmth
Creativity	Grace	Optimism	Wealth
Cunning	Gratitude	Organization	Wisdom
Dependability	Happiness	Passion	Zeal

Which of these speaks to you the most? Is there something important to you that is missing? There are no right or wrong answers, and this chart is in no way comprehensive. It's just a starting place. Use this list to begin to put words around your beliefs and values. As you put chits in your box, consider how they will influence your journey. Once you are clear on what your beliefs and values are, then you can have a better sense of whether or not the actions you are taking fit with those beliefs and values.

How Does Your Past Influence Your Beliefs and Values?

Your beliefs and values don't come out of thin air. They are influenced by and come from many sources of beliefs, such as environment, past experiences, events, knowledge, social media, and many others. An example of the most basic belief is the simplest form—that a given thing exists or does not exist. Your beliefs, especially your religious ones, are likely rooted in what your parents taught you. While it isn't uncommon for people to explore their own spiritual beliefs and convert to a religion that suits their own needs, for the most part, people whose parents are Christian remain Christian; people who were raised Muslim remain Muslim; and so on.

As I discussed earlier, certain beliefs are larger than religious ones. Political beliefs can be just as influential as religious beliefs. You may believe that the government has an obligation to take care of its economically disadvantaged citizens, or you may believe that is a duty best left to private charitable organizations. You may believe in a centralized federal government or more powerful local governments. You may believe that labor unions are a force for good or a force for evil. Your reason for believing these things is likely a result of your experiences.

Another form of belief is association, where A is like B or is related to A in some way. A example would be if you come from a family in which your father, and your father's father, and all your uncles were police officers, and you have had only good experiences with police officers. You are likely to believe, then, that police officers are generally good people who want to protect the community. If you come from a community, however, in which you don't personally know any officers, and you do know friends and neighbors who have been shot by officers when they were unarmed, you may believe that police officers are overly aggressive and not to be trusted. It's dangerous to make the assumption that things are the same, when, in reality, things are very different. In this case, we are equating A with B.

There is also the belief that "shit happens," and the world is imperfect; things ebb and flow as they change around us. We have a constant need to explain things and indicate cause as part of the explanation, which is causation. Another challenge is that we are not without bias, which causes us to place greater emphasis on ideas that support our beliefs. We selectively pick and choose the information that supports our positions, but we also skip over information that does not support our positions. These two opposing views are referred to as *confirmation bias* and *disconfirmation bias*.

The key point is simple: beliefs define an idea or principle that we surmise is true. There is nothing simple, however, about how our minds process beliefs. People hold on to their beliefs so vehemently that lives are routinely sacrificed or saved, based on what people believe. We often hear people profess complete certainty in the truth of their ideas, with no basis or sufficient evidence to support them.

There is a growing recognition and debate of how irrational our supposedly rational thinking can be. Many researchers who study the field of neuroscience highlight the complexity of the brain and its ability to attach to ideas, people, places, and things in rational and irrational ways. This concept of attachment is a heavy influencer in how much we believe or disbelieve an idea or thought. We become entangled in the vast set of emotions that are associated with what we believe to be true, and we violently reject what we believe to be false.

As you can see by the examples, the beliefs that we continue to build upon, bit by bit, spin a tangled web that causes us to validate and revalidate existing beliefs. This fight between confirmation and deconfirmation impairs our judgment to an extent that can be detrimental. While there are other theories around the types of beliefs, confirmation bias and disconfirmation bias are two of the most powerful.

All of your experiences, from the small (I was eating spaghetti on the day I had my first kiss) to the large (I was watching a rerun of *Friends* when I got the call that my mother had passed away), shape our feelings, thoughts, beliefs, and values. If a playground bully called us fat or ugly, we may be extra-conscious of our weight or looks. If we were praised as a child for our athleticism, that may be where we pride ourselves. The more we are aware of these things, the more we can check ourselves to see if the automatic assumptions we make about our beliefs and values are truly representative of who we are or if they are simply a reflection of outside forces.

ASSESSING OUR VALUES AND BELIEFS

Not all of our values and beliefs serve us well. Our parents, peers, and teachers, however well-intentioned, may not have always taught us lessons that allow us to reach our goals in productive ways.

Imagine that you grew up in a family that valued strength. This sounds like a good thing, and it can be. But if your family valued strength above everything else, and you were required to keep a stiff upper lip and not show weakness, that can be a problem. If asking for help when you needed help was considered a form of showing weakness, is that a helpful value to hold?

If your family valued academic achievement, that would be a great thing in a vacuum but not necessarily if you had a learning disability that made reading or math difficult or if your strength was in mechanical aptitude or the arts. You may be a talented plumber or auto mechanic or painter or dancer but a poor high school student.

Likewise, religious faith can carry you through dark times and give you a sense of purpose, value, and community. But if the tenets of that faith don't square with who you fundamentally are—for example, if you find yourself attracted to someone of the same sex or of a different race or religion, and your faith preaches against this—then those religious beliefs may prevent your growth. You may need to question why you hold those beliefs in order to fully become your own person. Do you believe them because you have been told, throughout your entire life, that you should, or do you believe them because you truly—deep in your soul—believe that they are true?

You are not the same person you were as a child. What was important to you at age five is not the same thing that was important to you at fifteen, and what was important to you at fifteen is not the same thing that was important to you at twenty-five. As you grow and learn and experience more of life and the world, your viewpoint shifts, and your beliefs and values may change as well.

Just because you were comfortable with a set of values and beliefs at one point in your life does not mean that you will remain comfortable with that set of values and beliefs for the rest of your life. As you mature, your values and beliefs will mature along with you.

There are no hard and fast rights and wrongs to values and beliefs. Whatever makes you comfortable, serves your purposes, and squares with your essential self is right for you. One of the biggest misconceptions people often harbor is that beliefs are static. This could not be further from truth! Beliefs are a choice. We have the power to choose our beliefs. Our beliefs become our reality.

It is a useful exercise to reexamine what is important to you and to question your own assumptions from time to time. You may find that you have made some radical shifts in your thinking. This may be because you have met someone who has opened your eyes to a new idea, or it may be because you have had an experience that has shifted your viewpoint. Or it may be something more subtle. Regardless, it is helpful to take a step back before you become dead set on your values and beliefs. It is helpful to periodically examine them by asking yourself:

- Why do I believe this?
- Why do I value this?
- How does this belief serve me?
- How does this value help me to become a better person?
- How does this help me achieve my goals?
- When I look into the mirror, do these beliefs and values describe what I see?
- Do these beliefs and values harm me in any way?
- Is there a way to hang on to the good in these beliefs and values, while removing the harmful parts of them?

The *challenging* part of challenging your values and beliefs puts everything in question. It puts everything at risk that you have been taught or have learned from others or that you have derived from an uninformed perspective. It will make you question everything, from God, to family traditions, to marriage, to raising children, to the social circle in which you belong. It's okay to leave an outdated belief behind. If you don't need it to take you where you want to go or if it is holding you back, let it go. If an old-fashioned value is preventing you from making progress in the modern world, leave it in the past.

We hold on to these things out of habit because we feel they are as much a part of ourselves as our arms and legs—but they aren't. They're more like fashion styles. What was fashionable in the 1980s might have gotten you to the front of the velvet rope at the club in 1985, but it isn't going to work today. A little black dress might be classic and never go out of fashion, but a leisure suit had its day and is never coming back. Keep your classics, and jettison those things that don't work anymore. Don't keep them in your closet. Get them out of your box and, thus, out of your life. They have no place there anymore—at least at this time.

You do not have to go on believing or valuing beliefs that were handed to you. You might not have been taught that you do get to choose. You can choose to remain with the status quo, or you may choose to rebuke it. The important thing is that you get to choose. The longer you take to understand that your beliefs and values create your reality, the longer it takes to reveal your true self. If you are wedded to believing someone else's beliefs or taking on someone else's values, then whose reality are you living? I would venture to say it's not yours.

It is within your power to choose what you value and what your beliefs are; this may be new to you. If it is, imagine creating your new reality, your new life, through eyes that are viewing things for the very first time. Take in the awareness of it all. But if you are in the midst of the shit that you have been shoveling for years, what do you do? How do you get yourself unstuck? What happens next will be based on your beliefs, values, actions, and behaviors. These are directly related to each other.

SELF-LIMITING BELIEFS

Self-limiting beliefs are the perceptions and assumptions that we make about ourselves and about how the world works. We refer to that as *self-limiting* because, in many cases, they hold us back. They are centered around beliefs about us, beliefs about others, and beliefs, more broadly, about the world. In many cases, these types of beliefs have a way of influencing the way we think, feel, and behave in a manner that is unproductive. Each of these beliefs can take on two dimensions. For instance, we may believe that the world is against us, that others wake up every day to ruin our lives. On the other hand, we may think the world supports us and that nothing can go wrong. It may be that we think we are the best and above everyone else. The flip side is that we think we are failures and incapable of succeeding. These are just two examples of how self-limiting beliefs become toxic and unhealthy, thus wreaking havoc on our lives. These unhealthy habits create unhealthy behaviors and negative outcomes.

This is why you must challenge your beliefs and create new, healthy ways to replace the unhealthy ways. Realize that your beliefs may not be completely accurate and may not represent a realistic perspective. Your beliefs can impact your ability to create more potential, or they can simply hijack your ability and drain your energy and focus. The key to taking control of these types of beliefs is to first identify and acknowledge them as self-limiting beliefs. Weeding out beliefs that are limiting can prevent you from getting stuck, eroding your self-esteem, and tumbling backward. Taking control is the way to empower yourself to reach your full potential. This can only be accomplished by choosing to work from the inside out and facing down the self-limiting beliefs.

Box Thoughts

1. Are your beliefs serving you well?
2. What are your self-limiting beliefs?
3. What values are important to you, and are they serving you well for forward progress?

CHAPTER 6

Heart, Mind, and Soul

THINK ABOUT WHAT YOU LEARNED IN HIGH SCHOOL ABOUT AN electrical circuit. To make a light bulb turn on, you had to connect a power source to the light bulb. To do this simple experiment on completing a circuit, you'd connect a battery, some wires, and a light bulb. If the filaments in the light bulb were burned out, the light would not turn on. If the wires connecting everything were severed, the light would not turn on. If the battery had no power, the light would not turn on. If everything was connected, you would have light.

Your heart, mind, and soul are the same way. All three need to be operational and connected in order for the light of your actions and behaviors to shine. If any one of these elements or components isn't working, the whole system shuts down. They don't work independently; they all work in concert with each other.

Briefly, let's talk about what the heart, mind, and soul are.

Our hearts are the center of our passions. It is where we love and feel. Our hearts are where we get excited about things and where we genuinely desire people, things, and outcomes. The heart is the center of our wants and desires. At times, our hearts can feel broken; they can ache and feel empty. When our hearts are full of love and life, it seems that we are running at full speed. Our hearts are not just central to keeping everything going physically; they also are central to our mental being.

Our minds are our rational and—at times—irrational thoughts. Our minds are the core of our reasoning, thinking selves. It is where we *know*. It is where we learn. It is where we wonder in amazement at new things and become challenged by the unknown. The mind is so astonishing that researchers still are amazed by its ability and capability. Our minds are powerful enough to store, process, retrieve, and use information. The mind is responsible for processing feelings and thoughts, yet it is the foundation of our imaginations.

Our souls are our spiritual cores. The soul is the most difficult to describe because it contains the unknown and unknowable. It contains our life essences and what makes us ourselves. It connects us to the greater universe. Many believe that our souls can transcend yet connect us at the deepest level.

ALIGNMENT

> Put your heart, mind, and soul into even your
> smallest acts. This is the secret of success.
> —Swami Sivananda

In chapter 5, I talked about making sure that the beliefs and values that you put into your box are those that will serve you well along your journey. In chapter 3, I talked about the value of promises and keeping your word. You have placed these beliefs and values in your box. You keep your promises, and people can rely on you to do what you say you are going to do. Now I'd like to talk about all of those things and how they interact with each other and with your actions and behavior.

It is important to understand that alignment is about how your actions and behaviors align with your promises, intentions, beliefs, and values. By examining all of these, you should be able to distinguish which ones serve your goals and aspirations.

This concept was first introduced to me in 2007. I was attending a training session at work, and they presented a session on alignment. What struck me about this session was that they provided a tool to help visualize how I could easily get out of alignment. Obviously, this session made an impact on me. I began examining my life by using this method to move beyond trying to find balance and to bring myself into alignment.

I really started to be more aware of my actions and behaviors. I tried to ensure that my beliefs, values, intentions, and promises were supporting my actions and behaviors. It also helped me to understand how the experiences led me to the next step in my journey. It helped me to gain control over the fear of the unknown and made it more exciting to step into unchartered territory.

Another thing that occurred over the years of practicing alignment was my ability to react differently to stress and to develop release mechanisms. The concept of alignment seemed simple, but it has required daily practice. You can very easily slip back into old habits and patterns that are comfortable. The key is to continue to challenge yourself by questioning your intentions every step of the way. I also learned to trust in the process of experiential learning. I found that every experience and encounter was a necessary part of the journey. I began to examine my beliefs, values, actions, and intentions in relation to my behavior. I focused on ensuring that the promises I made were kept—this was and is something that I value just as much as integrity. But I also learned that taking on things because I did not want to let someone down was more than just that. In the deepest part in practicing alignment, I found that making an impact was most important for me. If I was to be true to myself, everything that I set out to do needed to focus on making an impact.

Now, take a look at what you are doing. Is each action that you take in alignment with your beliefs and values? Is it a true reflection of what you believe and what you value? Does each action you take underscore your promises? Do all of these things add up to behavior patterns that align with the beliefs and values in your box?

These are not questions you can ask yourself once and be done. This is a constant check and recheck. When they are out of alignment, nothing will work. The gears of a watch must be in perfect alignment, or it will not keep good time; similarly, all of these aspects of your life must line up perfectly. You have to constantly tune up by checking in with yourself to ensure that you are in alignment, to make sure that you are working with precision, if you want to meet your goals.

WHAT HAPPENS WHEN YOU ARE OUT OF ALIGNMENT?

It's easy to say what happens when things are in alignment—they work! Everything goes smoothly and according to plan. But what happens when they aren't in alignment?

Your heart, mind, and soul are most affected when your actions, behavior, beliefs, values, and promises are out of alignment. This is obvious, when you think about it.

Think about the last time you did something you knew you shouldn't be doing. How did you feel? Did your stomach hurt? Did your gut tell you that you shouldn't be doing what you were doing? Did you know in your heart and soul that the action you were taking wasn't right?

Our bodies, minds, and souls respond when we aren't acting and behaving correctly. Some of us manifest physical ailments or pains. Some of us get that inner feeling of unease. Some of us feel spiritually sick. Many times, we don't even realize the effect that being out of alignment has on us, over the longer span. We may find ourselves in unhealthy situations or find that we are not happy in our professional and personal lives. We try to maintain a positive outlook.

We know what is right. Our instincts are generally good, but we talk ourselves out of them. We think our reason is where it's at, but often, our reason is nothing but a manifestation of fear or insecurity or the voices of others talking to us. If our intentions are pure, if our paths are clearly lighted, then we will know if we are on the right paths. When we sway and are out of alignment, everything breaks down.

Think of the tires on your car. If you have ever driven your car when it is in need of an alignment, you may have noticed a pull. This pull gets worse over time, if not addressed. You know that you need to keep the tires aligned, not just so the car will go straight but so that the rubber wears evenly and so you don't get dangerous bald patches. That pull is a sure sign that your alignment is off, and this is just like your life.

When things are out of alignment, you will notice this pull that seems to be working against you. You're trying to go one way but are being pulled in another. When your car is in alignment, it works better. You get better gas mileage, and your ride is safer if your tires are in alignment. It's the same for your body, mind, and soul; alignment is almost sacred to being able to achieve your innermost desires.

Likewise, people go to chiropractors to have their backs adjusted and aligned. When your spine, neck, and hips are aligned, it improves overall body function and performance. When these things are not aligned, you may experience back pain, leg pain, or neck pain. It can affect your posture, the way you walk, and your self-confidence. In this case, it can have a ripple effect through your body, causing other issues that then affect your mind and soul.

Even though your behavior, your values, and your actions are not physical, like your tires and your spine, it is still important to align them. Without proper alignment, the message—your intention, your goals, your ultimate raison d'être—cannot properly manifest itself. Your heart cannot give and receive the proper messages of love. Your mind cannot think rational thoughts. Your soul cannot remain pure and wholesome.

None of these things exists independent of the others. They all exist interdependently. Bread is not the same as flour, water, eggs, and yeast. The ingredients must be combined in the proper way, under the right conditions, for it to become bread. If you forget one of the most important ingredients, then instead of getting bread, you get an inedible mess. Without proper alignment—not including the right things—you will have the same result:

DON'T EXPECT PERFECTION

Don't expect that just because you have everything aligned that it will stay in alignment. Things do go astray from time to time. Even our best efforts sometimes fail.

The trick is not to set a standard of perfection that is unachievable. Recognize that sometimes things won't be in perfect alignment. Know when they are not aligned and work to get them back into alignment.

How do you do that? There is no auto mechanic, chiropractor, or professional baker to whom you can turn in order to realign your behavior, actions, promises, beliefs, and values. So what do you do when you find these core strengths out of line?

That's where your heart, mind, and soul come in.

The better you work at knowing your heart, mind, and soul, the better you will be at realigning your core strengths. To begin practicing alignment, you'll need to think about where you are today. Think about what is ahead of you. To change, you will need to take the first step into unknown territory, realizing that facing the unknown can be unnerving or even terrifying. You will need to let go of the fear and take the plunge. This is where the shift happens, and your inner soul will begin the release on the death grip. This process is best achieved while sitting, relaxing, or meditating, to let your mind roam. Regardless of which method you use, your mind needs to be open. For me, this often occurs when I am driving by myself. I frequently turn off the radio to be in complete silence, especially if it is early morning or late evening with minimal traffic. It is sometimes the place where no one can interrupt me or break my thoughts. Now, don't think that I zone out while driving—I don't—but that the feeling of total silence, with only the road ahead of me, is somewhat empowering. It is sometimes the place in which things come to me; it is a place where I am vulnerable and open.

As you get better at practicing alignment or doing what I call *alignment sensing*, you will notice a change. As you see the changes or shifts in yourself, others will also see the change. You will begin to trust that the process of alignment works.

Your Heart

What are your passions? Are your passions aligned with your behaviors and actions? Are you doing what you truly love? Are your promises made out of love or only out of a sense of duty and obligation?

Check in with your heart as you take action. When you make a promise, see if it is in alignment with what your heart is saying. The more you do this, the more it will become automatic, and you will instantly know if what you are doing is contrary to your heart's desire.

YOUR MIND

The older you get, the wiser you get—that is, if you take the time to learn from your mistakes and what you have observed. Everything you see and do is a learning experience. Compare what you are doing to what you know to be true. Is what you are doing consistent with what you believe to be accurate? If you dispassionately reason the facts in front of you, do you come to the same conclusion?

You will instantly know if something is illogical or doesn't match with the facts. Your mind is a powerful machine, but you need to exercise it, just like you exercise your body. You need to create new experiences, connections, and thoughts to challenge your mind to grow. Like everything else, practice makes perfect. The more you do this, the more it becomes a natural habit.

YOUR SOUL

We all have an inner spirit that defines the kind of persons we are. It may not be the result of a logical, reasoned set of beliefs but based on beliefs about the universe and world around us that we simply profess to be true. Sometimes this can be extremely powerful; for no particular reason, it resonates with our souls. We just know it. Likewise, when something is contrary to our essential soulful natures, we know that too.

Your soul controls your inner voice—we all have one. Learn to listen to that still, small voice within you. What is it saying? Is there something that gives you that excited feeling that you can't contain, and your heart just wants to jump out of your chest? Pay special attention; it will never steer you wrong. Once your mind is ready and tuned in to hear what comes your way, you will be open to receive. It's a matter of mindful listening.

Once you have practiced being in touch with your heart, your mind, and your soul—once you are truly aware of what your heart, your mind, and your soul consist of—you will know when an action or behavior is or is not in alignment with those core strengths. Even when you get good at it and it becomes instinctual, don't just ride on that instinct; constantly check in.

We learn and grow as we age. Our desires change; our minds change as the world changes around us. Having a periodic check-in will ensure that we stay in alignment so that we can achieve what we want to achieve. Do your alignment sensing.

Box Thoughts

1. Are your beliefs and values, actions and behaviors in alignment with your intentions?
2. How can you be more intentional?
3. Are your behaviors and actions aligned with your passion?

CHAPTER 7

Intentional Goals, Intentional Growth

IN CHAPTER 1 OF THIS BOOK, I TALKED A LITTLE BIT ABOUT MI-cro-goals and how they can make an insurmountable goal seem more achievable. Sometimes, when you have a long-term goal, it can seem so far off into the distance that it seems unattainable.

My relationship with setting goals is like being on a seesaw. One minute, I'm excited and ready to go, and the next minute, I have lost motivation. It is just like setting a New Year's resolution for a new goal, but then the next year rolls around without your goal being attained. The challenge with goal setting is that we tend to set goals that are either too far off or too small or narrow. But most of the time, we are unsure or not very clear in our goal setting.

This is the perfect time to assess whether your goals are focused on something you really want. We might waste time on goals that are meaningless or that are not designed to move us forward. Change is one of the hardest things to do, and it does not come without being intentional. Being intentional does *not* mean that you are unaware of the journey ahead of you; it means that the goal that you set today matters in the big scheme of things. While we tend to set large goals, we often don't think about what we need to do to achieve them. We put them on our vision boards or write them in our journals. For most, that is where they stay. They are like a big, one-eyed monster that stares at us and says, "You think you can take me on?"

When I work with others, I ask them to set big goals and then think about what they can do in the next month or two to move toward their big goals. Essentially, I ask them to break it down into smaller, bite-size pieces, which is where micro-goals come in.

ESSENTIAL ELEMENTS

> What we call little things are merely the causes of great things; they are the beginning, the embryo, and it is the point of departure which, generally speaking, decides the whole future of an existence. One single black speck may be the beginning of gangrene, of a storm, of a revolution.
>
> —Henri-Frederic Amiel

Nearly everything can be broken down into smaller elements. Your body can be broken down into its parts; your body parts can be broken down into cells; the cells of your body can be broken down into the parts of the cell, like the nucleus and the mitochondria; the parts of the cell are made up of atoms. Atoms are made up of protons, neutrons, and electrons. Beaches are made of grains of sand; mountains are made of individual pieces of soil.

The way to tackle anything overwhelming is to break it down into its essential elements. Anything can be scary if you take it as a whole. How do you eat a pizza? One bite at a time. How do you run a marathon? One stride at a time. How do you accomplish your goal? One micro-goal at a time.

Instead of looking at your entire ambition as a whole, create a series of micro-goals and focus on each of these essential elements as you do them. What do you want to do? Create a multi-million-dollar successful company? Write a series of novels? Get a medical degree? Each of these things can seem monumental when seen from a distance. But each individual step along the way is something that can be accomplished.

For example, when you set up a business, you first need to write your business plan. This involves not just the task of writing a business plan but researching the market, the cost of office space, supplies, staffing, and insurance. You have to come up with pricing and a timeline. A budget is helpful in figuring out how much money you need to begin. Then you have to figure out where that money will come from. All of these small steps are just some of the things you need to do before you ever hire your first employee.

It sounds like a lot but not when you look at the tasks one at a time. The list is long, but doing an internet search or calling rental agents to find out the cost of office space in your area is not very hard. That's one micro-task that you can do.

Micro-goals are a way of breaking this down. There will be a lot of hurdles between you and the end of the road—if the road ever ends. Remember the song from your childhood? "The bear went over the mountain, the bear went over the mountain, the bear went over the mountain, to see what he could see... he saw another mountain, he saw another mountain ... he climbed the other mountain ..." and so on. There's always another mountain to climb, another river to cross. What you think is the end of the road might just be the crest of the hill or the horizon.

A journey of a thousand miles begins with a single step.
—Lao Tse

INTENTIONAL GOALS

To begin your journey, you have to take that first step—setting your goal. But to continue your journey, you have to keep taking steps and setting new goals. The entire journey is made of many steps, and each step represents the work that you put in toward achieving your goal.

We need to focus on the end of our journeys so that we know where we are going, but intentionality requires us to ask several pertinent questions. Why do we want to achieve this? Is this our biggest priority right now? Does this align with our values? Will this make a difference in achieving our mega-goals? Will this matter in one month, three months, or six months?

Most of the time, we are not focusing on the step we are taking at the moment we are taking it. We are, instead, focusing on the incredible number of steps that need to be taken between now and then. That can feel overwhelming and derail our ability to take the next step.

Instead, be intentional about the step you are taking when you are taking it. The only step that matters is the one you are taking right now because being in the moment allows you to determine what that next step may need to be. Remember that this is not about filling your box with chits to make it full; it is about setting micro-goals that work toward something larger. You may set a goal to buy a new house but know that it will take you a long time to save the money and get positioned. The micro-goals that you may set might be saving 10 percent of your pay per month, researching the area where you want to live, and understanding the buyers' market.

Getting through all of this in a short period may be unrealistic and may not even be achievable, if you realize that you don't make enough income to purchase the home you want. You will then need to reassess your goals and be intentional about how you will work toward achieving the larger goal. You may need to look for another job or reassess your buying options. While this may seem simple for some, it is monumental for others.

You've likely heard the old phrase, "The road to hell is paved with good intentions." What does this mean? If our intentions are good, why aren't our paths good? Why aren't we heading to a good place?

It isn't enough that we mean well; we have to *do* well. This is why being deliberate and thoughtful—making sure that your actions and behaviors are in line with your heart, mind, and soul—is more important than meaning well.

As you put each chit in your box, don't just casually write it and throw it inside. Many experts highlight that goals must be specific and measurable. While there are many methods to evaluate your goals, I have found the SMART method the easiest to understand and follow. SMART stands for specific, measurable, achievable, relevant, and time. It requires you to ask yourself five questions. Is your goal *specific*? Can you *measure* your progress to know when your goal is achieved? Can your goal actually be *achieved*? Is your goal *relevant* to your desires? Can you establish a *time* in which it can be completed?

Be deliberate and intentional, but understand the big picture. Not understanding the big picture and losing focus on what you need to move forward can inadvertently sabotage your efforts. If your goals are intentional, you will achieve forward movement.

INTENTIONAL GROWTH

The big challenge is to become all that you have the possibility of becoming. You cannot believe what it does to the human spirit to maximize your human potential and stretch yourself to the limit.

—Jim Rohn

You may have experienced the feeling that your personal growth is similar to slogging through a mud pit or that you take one step forward, only to take two steps back. I can assure you that the challenges we experience and the obstacles we overcome all contribute to our personal growth. Realize that there will be times when things are not so pleasing, and it will seem like you are in a never-ending period of turmoil. Just remember that we must go through these times to become who we will become. Your world, my world, our world is filled with ambiguity, complexity, uncertainty, and volatility that requires us to be versatile, adaptable, and resilient. We can either sit back and wait for things to happen, or we can be intentional about our growth. We need to come to grips with the fact that if we don't design the lives we want—design our plans—it very likely will be done for us. We will then spend our lives living someone else's plan.

If you are living someone else's plan, the chances are you have not and will not reach your full potential.

We are not taught how to take care of our own growth early enough in life. We grow up having others take responsibility for our growth. Once we become young adults, this changes, and then we are solely responsible for our growth.

Has anyone ever given you a guide or advice on what you are supposed to do to ensure that you grow, personally and professionally? Are you in a job that you have grown to hate? Do you feel stuck, stymied, or just plain unhappy with your growth? You may have thought that if you did what you were asked, you would experience growth and forward motion. If you believe that growth will just happen, you may be greatly disappointed at the end of the day.

As with everything else, you need to be intentional about your growth. It will not happen automatically, and you will not just stumble upon it. Personal growth occurs over the length of your lifetime, and it is almost as if you get into a growth cycle that is spurred by the obstacles, goals, and actions.

Many experts that say personal growth and development happens in stages, but the consensus ends there. Some believe there are four stages, some believe there are six stages, and some believe in even more. After reviewing many different variations, the stages that were most important for my personal growth were more like stops along the way instead of stages. At various points in my life, I found myself progressing more in one role than another or more professionally than personally. At other times, it was the opposite, or all parts of my life grew in concert with one another. As you think about the different stages, realize that they don't happen in a linear fashion and may not be applicable to your life as a whole as new obstacles occur. You may be at different parts in the stages for your professional and personal lives. Regardless of how it unfolds for you, being intentional about your growth will help to ensure you stay in a learning mode. The main stages of personal development are as follows:

The first stage is about being unaware and unknowing. At this stage, you may get stuck at the starting line and don't move forward. You refuse to acknowledge what has been laid at your feet. It is denial, ignorance, naivete, self-destruction, and simply being stuck. If you are open-minded, curious for the unknown, and ready to take on the opportunities that will come your way, you can grow significantly during this phase. In fact, negative as well as positive experiences can contribute to your growth,

Awareness is the second stage and is truly where growth begins to open up. You become awakened to your reality and face it head on. You learn more about yourself in this phase, through discovery and understanding the things in your life around you. In this phase, you are attentive to your abilities, knowledge, ideas, successes, and overall potential that infuses your confidence in a manner that creates forward movement. It is still possible to get stuck in this phase if you are fearful, doubtful, or self-loathing or you distrust everything about yourself. You need to be mindful of the detractors and negativity that can poison your efforts.

The next stage is acceptance, which is about moving past the negative and allowing the positive to resonate and last far into the future, which is when true personal growth occurs as the result of change.

When I think of the power of acceptance, a recent situation comes to mind. I have several autoimmune issues that I have been dealing with for years. In 2018, I developed allergy-induced asthma. I had never had any type of asthma before that. This affected me so severely that walking fast or up the stairs became difficult. I hated walking with others when I had to tell them that I had to take the elevator to go up two floors. I tried to will it away. It really impacted my body, mind, and soul for a period of time. I finally realized that I might have to learn how to adjust in order to deal with it. Once I made the decision to learn how to live with it, it stopped being the first thing that popped into my mind, and it also stopped affecting how I felt about myself. It wasn't that I accepted the hand that was dealt to me, but I stopped allowing it to control me. I set new habits, goals, and patterns for myself to work through the tough times and to use the emergency inhaler when I need it. But most importantly, it made me focus more on my breathing, relaxing the muscles in my chest naturally, and easing into deeper, more controlled breaths. When it first happened, it was frustrating and made me feel weak. Once I learned to accept this new invader—learn to understand it and learn the triggers—the power of acceptance became a neutralizer and, at times, even transformational.

The next stage is focusing on taking matters into your own hands; take responsibility instead of waiting for fate to step in or for someone to come to your rescue. Responsibility is understanding that you are your own happiness; you can make the change, and you are in charge of your life. This stage can be empowering and can release you from so many things that may be holding you back. Taking responsibility for everything you do can be scary, but until you realize the power it gives you to move forward, you are being reactive instead of proactive.

This next stage is about applying what we learn, and it may be the most important for us to focus on. It is about setting macro- and micro-goals. It is about taking action. Many of us get stuck at a particular stage, but this stage is probably the most likely place that people get stuck. In fact, they can get paralyzed to the point that it affects their emotional states. At this stage, you must focus on self-discipline, as well as focusing on your goals and, most of all, being motivated. This is also the point when you must gain clarity about your goals and what is in front of you. Getting stuck at this stage can quickly set off a vicious cycle of doing the same thing expecting different results.

The last stage is all about purpose and being intentional about our growth. You must think about becoming a perpetual learner so that you can keep growing. This is the stage in which habits and mind-set are important for fueling continued growth. You must live with purpose—being your best, doing your best, and being aware, as well as developing a level of awareness that allows you to transcend obstacles. Continued growth and learning and challenging yourself is not easy. It is hard work but can be amazingly rewarding. Learn to reassess, accept, seek change, and crave growth. The more you learn how to leverage the stages of growth, the more you will be able to be intentional with your growth.

INTENTIONAL STEPS EQUAL INTENTIONAL GOALS

While you are working toward each micro-goal, be intentional with it. Focus on who, what, and where you are, and be mindful of what you are doing. Recognize the importance of focusing on the task at hand. If you take each micro-goal seriously and intentionally, one at a time, you will take an intentional step toward your goals.

Each intentional step you take gets you that much closer to your goal. If your steps are intentional, the goal you reach will be intentional. There's a difference between getting in the car and seeing where the road takes you and having a definite route in mind. The journey may look the same out the window of the car, but the end result will be quite different.

Writing a novel is difficult; typing each individual letter or word is not. Though the micro-goals look the same, writing any old word won't result in a good book; choosing each word with care and intention will result in a book you can be proud of.

When you are intentional and deliberate with each micro-goal, even though you may not be much further towards your goal, you can be assured that you will get there. Choose each micro-goal that you place in your box with an eye toward alignment with your values and beliefs. Each micro-goal must align with your heart, mind, *and* soul.

Here's the thing: when you do this, you not only have reached your esteemed goal, but you have achieved a greater self. Your intentional steps lead to intentional goals. Those intentional goals lead to intentional growth. You will increase your wisdom and knowledge. Your ability to capture the spirit around you will expand.

Box Thoughts

1. What are you doing to bring intentionality into your life?
2. What are the biggest challenges impacting your growth?
3. How can you set more achievable goals?

CHAPTER 8

Visualize and Validate

Belief in the unknown and unknowable is progress.

IT IS HARD TO IMAGINE ACCOMPLISHING A GOAL WITHOUT—WELL, without first imagining it. The greater and more detailed your imagination and your picture of what you want to do, the more likely you will be to fully realize your goal. Think about someone who is successful. How much hard work did that person put into his or her goal? No matter whether it is professional or personal, the key thing is to start with a goal. It doesn't matter whether it is a big or small goal. Our goals become our guides and compasses; they give us purpose. But none of it is possible without hard work and strong determination.

My goal is to help you develop a clear, practical set of goals, objectives, or ideas that focus on building the life you want. It is also my goal to get you to challenge any preconceived notions you may have on what is necessary to achieve your goal.

Before you can establish goals or set things in motion, perhaps the most important thing is to have some idea of what *it* will look like. You must be able to visualize and create a mental picture of your future, yourself, and your life. Without taking the time to visualize what you desire, you won't be able to see the possibilities.

People may tell you, "Think it, and you will become it." I wish I could say it is that simple. In fact, athletes, professionals, students, and many others have used visualization techniques, based on research and science, to pursue and achieve their goals. Many people use visualization to improve motivation, behavior, and concentration and to fuel forward movement.

Using visualization to see our actions causes the brain to go through the same pattern of firing up neurons as if we were performing the action—just as the action creates a new neural response, thus triggering our memories as well as behaviors, visualization triggers the same response.

This is why vision boards have become popular in leadership seminars. Grown-ups, especially executives with high-powered jobs, might feel silly cutting pictures out of magazines and pasting them on a poster board, like they are making a project for the third-grade science fair. But it is more than that. It isn't enough to say, "I want to be something." There is something powerful about having an actual, representative picture of what you want to be and where you want to go and being able to look at it for inspiration.

The more specific your vision, the more complete your picture of what you want and the more likely you will be to realize what you have visualized. If you only have a fuzzy image of what you want to achieve, then your ultimate achievement likely will be unclear as well. The more definition you have, the better. In taking visualization a step further—and to get the most of it—you will need to use two types: *outcome visualization* and *process visualization*.

Outcome visualization is used to visualize not just the goal but achieving the goal. Process visualization is used to visualize the actions that are necessary to achieve the desired outcome. Using the chit as a mechanism to help you visualize your goal is a powerful way to create a positive change in behavior, as well as designing the life you want.

It is also important to realize that while you are embarking on your journey, there will be times when things will get tough, or you will get down on yourself. Get in the habit of asking yourself what you need now to move forward.

When we are hesitant or are unsure of ourselves, we seek validation from others. When we have experienced something challenging or troublesome, we seek input from others. Why do we seek others' validation of whether we did something right or are good enough? Why do we look to someone else to see the best in ourselves? Many times, we are quick to reject our thoughts, ideas, and feelings when we get frustrated or angry because things aren't going our way or when things are spinning out of control. We need to avoid judging ourselves, take a step back, and allow ourselves to feel the way we feel.

Don't tell yourself how you *think* you should feel; just feel. Pretend you are someone else talking to you, and comfort yourself the way you would comfort a friend in need. Be kind to yourself. Think about your accomplishments and strengths, and show yourself gratitude with positive reinforcement, rather than diving into negative self-talk. While it is great to get praise from others, it is more important for you to value yourself by praising yourself. Don't fixate on the negativity or allow doubt and uncertainty to paralyze you. You don't need someone else's permission to feel proud about who you are and what you are doing. It is your life; thus, it is your box. Design it and create it, based on your unique self. Allow your box to help you strive to be the best *you* that you can be.

WHAT DOES YOUR BOX LOOK LIKE?

Let's start with your box. Let your imagination run wild. You will need to consider how big it is, what it looks like, and what it is made out of. There are no right or wrong answers. This is your box and your vision. As long as it suits your needs and your desires and as long as it fits with your intentions, it is perfect.

How big is it? Is it a steamer trunk, able to carry nearly everything you own? Is it something built into your wall, to be hidden behind a painting so that only you know where it is? Is it sized to sit on a display shelf so everyone can see it? Is it small, so you can carry it with you wherever you go?

What is it made of? Do you prefer something strong like steel? Solid like wood? Perhaps you want a box made of precious metal. You might want a delicately carved jade box. Something indestructible and fun to decorate, like melamine or Bakelite, might be more to your tastes.

What does it look like? Is it stately and solid-looking? Is it jewel-encrusted? Shiny? Painted with geometric shapes? Painted with pictures representative of things that are important to you? Decoupaged with whimsical designs? Sparkly? Carved? Inlaid?

How does your box open? Does it have a hinged lid? If so, what do the hinges look like? Are they big and metal, or are they hidden? Is there a trick to opening it? Are there latches? Do you need a key or a combination? Do you lift the lid off in its entirety? Do you open it from the side or the top?

The key thing is to develop a clear vision of your box. Give serious thought to what you want your box to reflect. Your box should be something that speaks to you, something that, when you look at it, you think about your life. Remember that you are the creator, the designer of your journey, the designer of your future. While it starts with this simple gesture of designing your box, it is so much more. This is taking a first step to making the change necessary to create the future you want.

WHAT'S IN YOUR BOX?

Now that you have a clear vision of your box and how it opens, close your eyes, and picture that box in your mind. Make sure you can see it from all sides. Lift it up, turn it over, and examine it. Now, put it down, and open it up. What will you put inside it?

Is your box "a box of nothing," like that box I got at the party all those years ago, which started my thinking? The box, when it is empty, still has meaning. It represents unlimited potential. I remember that I thought I would take that "box of nothing" and fill it with something. You too can fill your empty box with something. But also remember that when I got the box, there was something in it—a paper that was a summary of someone's accomplishments. In reading that slip of paper, I thought about how we do so many things that have so little impact. I started thinking about what I would highlight as accomplishments—would they be things that moved me closer to my dream?

As soon as you place something in your box, it becomes filled with meaning. The challenge will be in deciding what kind of meaning you will put in your box. What true wishes and goals do you want to achieve? Will you focus on your career, education, health and wellness, or family? Will you work on defining your values and beliefs that you want as reflective of your future? Or will it be a combination of all of these things?

You can place anything you desire to achieve in the box, and the box can be anything you want it to be. The important thing is that your box is meaningful and that it is *yours*. It represents a choice—your choice. What you place in your box matters. That is what gives your box meaning. The box itself isn't meaningful—it might be one of a thousand that can be purchased at any retail store. It is the contents of the box that matter.

The title of this book isn't *What Kind of Box Do You Have?* It is *What's in Your Box?* This is because it's what is in your box that's important; it gets you focused on defining what you want your future to look like. Imagine the box as the vehicle for driving you to your destination. The contents are that gas that makes it possible to move.

STEPPING OUTSIDE YOUR BOX

> Step so far out of your comfort zone that
> you forget how to get back.
> —Anonymous

What do routines and boundaries have in common? They both are contributors to your staying in your comfort zone. We all have different boundaries, and we may feel lost without them. Boundaries provide us a false sense of security in our life journeys. In many cases, it goes against our natures to color outside the lines and to step outside the boundaries. This mind-set began in childhood, when our parents established boundaries to provide the much-needed structure that we craved as children.

As much as children may fight with their parents and rebel against their parents' rules, it is a psychologically proven fact that children thrive in structured environments. They need to know where the boundaries are and how they fit within those boundaries in order to feel safe and secure.

As adults, we are conditioned to operate within a given set of boundaries. It's funny that we establish those boundaries for ourselves. Because we set our own boundaries, we often set them a little bit too tightly, just to be on the safe side. Especially with the more risk-averse among us, stepping outside those boundaries can become scary. The older we get, the more we become comfortable and set in our ways. If we have found a way that works for us, even if it is imperfect, we stick with it.

When we do this, there is no growth. It is uncomfortable to step beyond the boundaries we have set for ourselves. It is called a *comfort zone* for a reason—it is comfortable! We tell ourselves that it is more than just comfortable. We tell ourselves that our hearts and our minds want us to stay in our comfort zones, that to leave these comfortable places is to step out of alignment with our core strengths.

Stepping outside isn't always stepping out of alignment. Discomfort isn't always the same as going against your gut. Fear isn't the equivalent of wrong. Sometimes you have to go around a blind corner; otherwise, you are always going to stay on the same block. While being in your comfort zone is low-risk and low-anxiety, you need to find your own ability to be productively uncomfortable.

If you stay where you are, you may remain comfortable, but you -also will stay where you are. Comfort kills forward movement, and frankly, that won't be comfortable. Again, I want you to close your eyes and visualize something you constantly avoid doing— whether it's sticking with an exercise plan, meeting new people, taking a much-needed course, or having a difficult conversation. Think about how much energy and effort you expend in trying to reshuffle things to avoid doing it. Think about what it feels like to remain in that place. That's the comfort zone. Think about never leaving the neighborhood where you live. You spend day after day, going no farther than the boundaries of your neighborhood. But then one day, you have to travel to a place you have never been— maybe flying for the first time. How did you feel? Were you anxious, excited, or stressed? That is being out of your comfort zone.

You cannot stay in the same place. You must be willing to take risks, regardless of how big or small, in order to move gradually toward your dreams. You cannot rest on your laurels because it is comfy or easy. Remember that *easy* is not where the seeds of success grow. If you want to achieve success, you have to go out of your comfort zone. Success and achievement—however you define it—is beyond the limitations of your comfort zone. Your response to life is paramount to the level of growth you will experience.

One of my favorite sayings is a slight twist on another saying: "If you want to run with the big dogs, you have to get off the porch." You must think big and dream big—go big, or go home.

USE YOUR HEART

How do you know if those negative feelings you have are simply fear of the unknown or a warning that what you are thinking about doing is out of alignment with your core values? Is the answer to use your heart? Is it to use your passion to guide you? The thing about using our hearts, which many of us don't understand, is that it is situational decision-making, if employed with a level of thoughtfulness and agility. Think about the types of decisions we encounter and the speed in which those decisions need to be made. We are more likely to make a bad decision when we are limited on time. We tend to do what I call *rush to failure*. When we are asked to make decisions based on the heart, we have to be able to sink below the surface of the iceberg. We need to get below the turbulent thoughts of fear, anxiety, noise, and emotions. Most of us are afraid of making the wrong choice and end up on the road to indecision. Do you realize that no decision is a decision? Many times, this indecision is clouded with self-doubt and uncertainty that causes our stress and anxiety levels to rise.

Have you ever been in the midst of contemplating what to do when your heart started racing, your palms got sweaty, your thoughts went crazy, and you knew you needed to decide what to do? How would you handle that situation? How would you calm your mind and know the right way to go? How can you hear what your heart is truly saying? How do you get past the doubt and fear?

You know where you ultimately want to go. You know what you love; you know where your passions lie. This is not something that anyone else can tell you. The question, then, is not whether what you are doing is frightening or uncomfortable but whether it serves your passion. Think about it: you make hundreds of choices daily as you go about your normal routine. You do this in a mindless manner—it's habit; it's second nature, and you don't even think about it. Why, then, when bigger, more important choices come forth, do we seem to spiral out of control? It is usually because it is territory into which we have never ventured. It is something new, different, or maybe more complicated than we have previously experienced.

Consider this: you might be afraid of speaking in front of a crowd. But your passion is bringing your product to the marketplace, and you can't do that without getting investors, which will allow you to manufacture the first batch. You can't get investors without talking to investment groups. You may tell yourself that talking to groups isn't something you are good at. You tell yourself that you will find other ways of finding financing. You decide to continue to do the same thing, thus getting the same results. In this situation, your fear is overriding all else. What do you do? Do you sit behind a computer screen, doing the same unsuccessful things you've been doing, hoping an investor will find you? Do you send out mass emails but don't go to the next step of doing a pitch to a group of investors? Does speaking to this group of investors scare you to death? Yes. Is it miles outside your comfort zone? Of course. But will it lead you to the success of your passion? Absolutely.

Instead of looking at the big, hairy problem as a monster, break it down, think about situations when you have tackled parts of this, and then think about the new things that you have not tackled. What is your heart telling you to do? It is probably screaming *yes*; it is probably putting you in motion until you get to the door. Then panic and fear set in. What are you feeling at that moment? Write it down. Take a mental note. Pause, breathe, calm yourself, and just sit with what makes your heart race. Is there a way you can learn this skill? Maybe it would be less dauting if you joined a Toastmasters group or a group that helped you refine and practice your pitch. Maybe you could do more research to figure out a way to accomplish presenting to investors, which moves you forward. Maybe you could practice your speech in front of a mirror or a group of trusted friends.

You know what you love. You know what your passion is. Your heart will not lie to you if you listen. Your mind, on the other hand, might lie to you, if it's not balanced with your intuition. What you think is the reason, might actually be fear speaking. Fear can get in your brain and pretend to be justification. Fear can sound reasonable and rational. Fear can immobilize you from reaching your full potential.

You will also know what you don't love. If what you must do is something that you dislike intensely, something that makes you sick to your stomach, you will know. You will know if you'd rather pull the covers over your head and stay in bed. If it feels like drudgery, or a chore, or a means to an obligatory end, it isn't serving your passion.

Take that much-needed pause or time-out. This is the perfect place to visualize, validate, and affirm by saying your goals out loud. I find that saying it to myself, then out loud and sometimes to others, helps to influence my thoughts in a manner that has a very natural effect. Affirmation of what your heart is saying is powerful. Don't just listen to your heart; affirm what your heart is saying. Your heart always knows what belongs in your box.

Box Thoughts

1. What does your life look like in five years, ten years, fifteen years?
2. What would it take for you to practice visualization on a daily basis?
3. Do you need constant validation? Once you have it, how does it make you feel?

CHAPTER 9

The Three Rs

Recover from the past, replenish today,
and reinvigorate for tomorrow.

I THINK I'VE MADE IT CLEAR THAT HAVING A BOX IS NOT A SIMPLE solution; it is another tool to help you design the life you want. It doesn't do away with hard work or effort. It only makes sure that all your hard work and effort are focused and productive and geared toward your passion.

Whenever you work hard, you will get tired. Sometimes, you may even be exhausted—perhaps you feel too exhausted to go on. You've accomplished a lot of your micro-goals, but there are still a lot of them left in your box before you can accomplish that massive goal. It just seems so far away, and you're not sure if you can keep going. You're not sure what is in sight for you, and you are starting to second-guess yourself. Essentially, you are in a state of stress, which is natural, as well as necessary, at times.

It seems that these days, things move so quickly, and with the advances in technology, we are accessible, exposed, and connected, twenty-four/seven. We seem to be constantly in the fight-or-flight mode, which can be very harmful to our reaching our full potential.

I bring this up because some of us push ourselves, sometimes to the point that we border on breaking. We forget that our brains and bodies need to recover and to be replenished and reinvigorated.

That's where the three Rs come in: recover, replenish, and reinvigorate.

We have to work hard to make progress, but working hard isn't the same as working constantly. There is nothing wrong with taking the time to recover when we need it—to replenish our energy in our own individual ways. We must do what we need to do to reinvigorate the energy that started us on our journeys. This is not just about dealing with the daily stressors; when we get to the point of exhaustion, our bodies simply don't function as well as they should. In many cases, when this happens, we stall, progress stalls, and stagnation sets in.

GETTING STUCK

Let's face it: no journey worth taking is ever smooth. When we see the people we admire sitting on their thrones of success, we only see the end result. We don't see their moments of frustration, the challenges they faced, or their stumbling blocks. I often speak about my journey and lessons learned because I want people to know that any level of success comes with all the things that life throws at us. Very few of us are given the silver spoon, the golden pass to no problems.

Everyone gets stuck at some point along the way. Often, when we are stuck, it can be draining because it comes in different forms. Our lives can be very complicated and full of so much stuff. We are so focused on our goals and everything we need to do to achieve them that everything else falls away.

This can be dangerous. This kind of hyper-focus is what leads to burnout. It is important to remember our friends and our families and our lives outside of our ambition. *Self-care* seems almost like an overused phrase these days, but the fact that it gets used a lot doesn't make it any less important.

It's important to pause, take that much-needed mental break, and use the three Rs. When your car gets stuck in the mud, if you just press on the gas, you will only grind the tires further into the mud. You need to get out and try something else. This is no different. Get out of your head from time to time. Clear your thoughts. Walk around. Get a fresh perspective. Breathe some different air.

You have to keep moving. If you stay stuck, you will inevitably stay where you are. You have to figure out a way to get out of the trap you are in. Staying there and spinning your tires is the worst way to do it. You will keep getting more and more stuck.

Using the three Rs is the best way to keep moving forward. Taking a short break is not the same as giving up. You need to take the time to recover, replenish, and reinvigorate in order to recharge your mental and physical bank. If you are too exhausted to perform, your performance won't be ideal. Even race car drivers stop racing to refuel. Without gas, your vehicle—your body, your mind, your spirit—can't continue to perform.

USING THE THREE RS

Everyone has a different way of recovering, replenishing, and reinvigorating. Extroverts find social events and crowds energizing; introverts find them exhausting. Introverts need alone time in order to recharge their batteries; extroverts find alone time boring and restlessness-making. There is no right or wrong to this; it is whatever works for you.

Make sure you take care of your physical health. You might think that pushing through in order to complete a project is the way to go. But are you really doing your best work when you are battling the flu? Are you thinking properly when your brain is feverish or when half of your brain is occupied with trying to keep your lunch contained in your stomach? You would be better off by taking a day or two to sleep and heal yourself. When your health is better, your work will be more efficient and effective.

Preventive methods also are important. You might think you don't have time to exercise, but taking a few hours a week to go to the gym, or take a walk, or go to a yoga class, or whatever suits you is a whole lot less time-consuming than a several-month leave of absence to recover from a cardiac event.

A lot of ambitious people ignore mental health concerns. They might see burnout as something that happens only to weaker people. If they do, they do so at their own peril. This isn't to say that everyone needs to take psychotropic medications (although certainly take them if you need them) or that you should be in therapy once a week (although, again, do so if you need it). Just take the time to care for your mind, just as you care for your body.

Take a class to keep your mind sharp. Have you always wanted to learn Spanish? Take a class at a local community college. Want to paint? Find a class at an arts center. Audit a history class at a university, if that's what interests you. It doesn't matter. If you have a curious mind, feed that curiosity.

Perhaps you have trouble relaxing. Then go for a massage. Massage therapy isn't just an indulgent thing for people who like to pamper themselves—not that there is anything wrong with a little pampering from time to time (you've worked hard; you deserve it). Massage therapy can help decrease back pain, increase blood flow and circulation throughout the body, and help with issues like headaches and trouble sleeping.

Take a vacation. Remember that scene in *The Shining* where

Jack Nicholson, as Jack Torrance, types over and over, "All work and no play makes Jack a dull boy"? There's some truth to that. While, hopefully, we won't be driven as homicidally insane as Jack Torrance, all work and no play can render us empty shells of our creative selves. We can't have perspective if we remain inside.

If you have ever watched an artist work with oil paints, you may have been surprised to see that their brushes often have very long handles. You might think that they would want to get up very close to their work to see the details, but often, the opposite is true. They need to stand back as far as they can when they work so they can see the bigger picture. They need to get different perspectives so they see how their brush strokes fit in to what they are doing.

Novelists sometimes work similarly. Sometimes, the best thing writers can do is put their works-in-progress in a desk drawer and walk away. Coming back to it a week, a month, or a year later can give them the needed perspective they need to fix whatever problem they had with what they were working on.

Vacations can be your long brushes or desk drawers. Getting a little distance from your work and your life might be all you need. Lying on a beach, or bungee jumping, or exploring ancient ruins or art museums might not seem like productive work, but that might be the recovery, replenishing, and reinvigorating your body and mind need in order to work properly. Getting that distance from the everyday slog of your work might give you the perspective you are looking for to solve that tricky knot of a problem that has you stuck.

When you wake up in the morning, how do you feel? What is the first thing you think about? Do you wish that you were ending the day instead of getting started? Do you dread the day that is ahead of you? Do you wake up feeling exhausted or well rested? Are there things that you should be doing less of or more of? What would it take to get you unstuck and into forward movement? How true are you staying to your authentic self?

In gaining perspective on where you are in your journey when things seem to be somewhat chaotic, the best place to start is to look at where you are, here and now. I love to use a catchy tune to light up my day. One of my favorites, when I need a reminder, is Janet Jackson's "Made for Now." This song reminds me, every time I hear it, to focus on where I am today. It makes me think that I was made for the moment that I am in. It reminds me that the secret to reinvigorating me is within me.

A full transformation is not always necessary to get unstuck and move forward. Sometimes, it is as simple as taking inventory of what you need to keep, let go of, or simply stop doing. Make a list of these things by jotting them down into the three categories. This is a good place to revisit your intentions, actions, and behaviors. This simple yet important exercise may take you several minutes, hours, or even days to create. Take the time you need to work through it. You may need to find a place of comfort or someplace that inspires you to really get into the space to face this head on.

What do you need to let go of? Are there things that are weighing you down or making you frustrated? What things are you doing that are counterproductive or that have a negative impact on your personal and professional lives? What are you doing that has a positive impact on your personal and professional lives? What things are working well in your life, and how can you do more of them? What are your strengths that make everything soar? Are there things that you should be doing that you are not doing? What actions can you take to enhance your life? Is there something you can do to get over the fear? What are some ways you can overcome the obstacle in your way? What opportunities exist as a result of the challenge? These are questions for you to consider when looking for the inspiration and perspective in order to be clear about your own potential.

Clearing the clutter around you and reinvigorating yourself with things that energize and inspire you will unlock your potential. This gives you the space to move more than you think. Fill your day with things that invigorate you, and limit those things that drain you. This may require you to change your focus, leverage your strengths, and seek to build opportunities. If you are waiting for that perfect opportunity to come, you may be waiting a long time. You need to build it, create it, and live it. Challenge yourself.

You need to be in a space in your life where you can be open, aware, and present to receive what comes your way. This also gets back to being intentional with your beliefs, values, actions, and behaviors. Focus on those things that are going right, that make you feel energized. Spend time finding ways to integrate invigoration into your daily habits. Use the three Rs to pull you out of that dark space and bring you into the light. Take care of yourself—because nobody else will.

Box Thoughts

1. What is the first thing you do when you get stuck?
2. How do you recover and replenish your energy when things are really tough?
3. Do you periodically work on a plan to reinvigorate yourself?

CHAPTER 10

Getting Out of Your Head

OUR THOUGHTS ARE AMAZINGLY POWERFUL. USING POWERFUL thoughts allows us to manifest our goals and dreams. The challenge for most of us is to manage the time we spend in our own heads. The worst part of being in our heads is that we can't shut our minds off, and our thoughts, no matter how we try clear them, keep coming. While the mind is actually doing what it is supposed to do, we allow our thoughts to run rampant and control how we show up.

We need to realize that thoughts often become our reality, both good and bad. In order to manage the chaos, we need to practice being in the moment and taking control. If we learn to harness our thoughts, we will be more successful in using them to achieve our goals. The main problem is that many of us can't manage our thoughts in a way that is useful. We get stuck in the think-sort-create cycle.

We think and think and overthink things for way too long. We worry about the things that we can't control, and those things dominate our thoughts. Or we get stuck in the past, reminiscing about what we should have done differently or should have said or could have said. We create a snowstorm out of random flurries. We tend to oversimplify or let the noise cloud our judgment. We become our own worst enemies.

When we were children, the people we wanted most to avoid were the bullies. No one wanted to hang around the mean kids— the kids who would call us names or make us feel ugly or clumsy or stupid. No one wanted to be with someone who made us feel incompetent or that we didn't know what we were doing. No one.

In adulthood, bullies still exist, but they are more subtle. Unfortunately, they aren't as easy to avoid, and you can't just sit at a different table in the cafeteria or play in a different place on the playground.

Mainly, the adult bullies are hard to avoid because we carry them around within ourselves. The most harmful negativity that we hear as grown-ups is inside our own heads. The source for most of our negative thinking is ourselves.

Think about your own internal dialogue. If you heard someone saying mean things about your best friend or your children that you say to yourself, wouldn't you be angry at that person? We may think that making derogatory comments to ourselves is not a problem; we may think this doesn't hurt anyone. But this could not be farther from the truth.

A number of behaviors, which we have discussed in previous chapters, contribute to our sabotaging ourselves. Internal behaviors that create problems and issues in our lives are factors in self-sabotage. We are not necessarily aware of our actions and behaviors that lead to self-defeating consequences. We also aren't aware of how those behaviors and actions undermine our forward progress. Even if we do recognize the behavior, how many of us actually stop the negative thinking?

Here are few examples of how this may show up in your life:

- negative beliefs about yourself
- preconception bias
- self-selecting out
- procrastination
- fear of success
- quitting when things get tough
- dwelling on too many options
- gossiping
- living in the past
- remaining powerless and speechless
- controlling things and people
- trying to please everyone

This is not a comprehensive list, but it should give you an idea of the signs to look for. Learning how to reverse self-sabotaging habits can free up a lot of personal energy. The key thing is to realize when you are getting in your own way.

Think about it. How many times have you looked in the mirror and criticized the way you look? How many times have you looked over your work and thought it was second-rate or not as good as it should be? How many times have you second-guessed yourself? How many times do you sabotage yourself in a day, week, or month? Are you your own worst bully? Do you suffer from imposter syndrome?

SELF-SABOTAGE

Why do we do this to ourselves? Hundreds of psychological books and articles have been written on this topic, and we still can't seem to make sense of why our conscious and subconscious minds turn our heads into a personal battleground, filled with alien thoughts. We begin to lash out by shutting in those feelings that drive us into survival mode. This mode is driven by fear and is focused on protecting ourselves from harm. Our minds sometimes fool us into believing there is a real, physical threat, when in reality it is coming from our own beliefs and experiences.

We talked previously about how our beliefs may not serve us well. This also applies to how we think about ourselves. In fact, many of us may harbor past experiences or internalize those things that were directed toward us as children. We fall victim to our own inner voices, and in order to protect ourselves, we often engage in self-sabotaging behavior. While our subconscious voices are formed from our early experiences, and we can't change the past, we can identify self-sabotaging thoughts and take action against them. Not addressing or taking action against them often leads to our exhibiting the same behavior; thus, we get caught in the cycle of unproductive behavior. This will instill fear and keep us from getting what we want in life.

In a nutshell, most of us who are driven to succeed are afraid of failure. This fear of failure makes us afraid to try anything at which we may fail. Criticism from people we respect stings. If we only reveal perfection, then we can't be criticized.

Nothing earthly, however, is perfect. So we focus on the flaws, however tiny, and not on everything else that is good. These flaws become magnified and are all we can see. Remember when we talked about perspective in chapter 9? We only see the one tiny, imperfect brushstroke and not the entire beautiful picture. That's why we need the paintbrushes with the long handles, so we can step back, get some perspective, and see the whole thing.

Our subconscious minds are trying to protect us from perceived harm and potentially deep-seated fear. This eventually results in preventing us from seizing new opportunities and accomplishing our goals, as well as our dreams.

You have to get out of your own head. Your head is a box, of sorts, of your own creation. It is filled with your values and be-liefs, but not all of them are productive. Many of them come from negative experiences you've had in your youth. Were you a victim of a childhood bully? Did you have overly critical parents? Or could you simply not please that teacher you respected?

You are the product of your past, but you are not carved out of stone. You can take the time to look at *why* you think the way you think. Take out that long paintbrush. Put that novel in the drawer. Take three steps away, and look at what you are doing.

Have you ever looked at a photograph of yourself from many years ago and, for a moment, before you recognized yourself, had an uncritical thought about yourself? Or maybe you caught yourself in a mirror in a strange hallway that you didn't know was there. Before you knew you were looking at yourself in a mirror, what did you think of that image? Think about it: we are capable of thinking our children are beautiful, even recognizing that our children look a lot like us, but we have a hard time labeling ourselves as beautiful. Why is this?

When you are *inside*, you can't see what something looks like from the outside. If you are inside a house, you can't say what the outside of the house looks like.

Get out of your own head to set yourself free from your self-imposed limitations.

IMPOSTER SYNDROME

Have you ever had that feeling that you are not enough, that you are not good enough, that you don't deserve to be promoted, or that you don't deserve to be where you are? Well, if you have, you're not alone—and you may be suffering from imposter syndrome. Imposter syndrome is a phenomenon where perfectly competent people feel like they are faking it and that it is only a matter of time before everyone else figures out that they are just imposters. They feel that their successes and achievements are nothing short of luck and that they are only fakers. They devalue their worth and undermine their very existences. Their thinking is, of course, erroneous.

Regardless of your level of success, if you experience feelings of inadequacy, self-doubt, and a sense of intellectual fraudulence, it is a sign you have imposter syndrome. This can apply to anyone who is unable to own his or her success. These feelings are only insecurities rearing their ugly heads.

We create these thoughts and feelings entirely within ourselves. Therefore, we have the power to banish these thoughts and feelings. There is no single reason why some of us experience imposter syndrome, but experts believe that our childhood memories are a key contributor. It is perfectly normal that we experience moments of doubt, but because we are the creators, we can be the destroyers.

SELF-SELECTING OUT

The term *self-selecting out* is most commonly used in statistical research, where your results would be severely affected by self-selection bias for many different reasons. More and more, however, this phrase is used in the workplace and also is used as a recruiting and hiring method. Self-selection is designed to provide an individual with the information necessary to make an informed decision on whether to apply for a job or opportunity. Some individuals make the best of this by seeking a new opportunity, but it is problematic when individuals self-select out before ever knowing if the opportunity is right for them.

If we are asked to consider an opportunity, we may get excited about it, but then we talk ourselves out of it before we even give it a chance. We begin to doubt ourselves; we don't allow ourselves to dream. We think of all the reasons why we can't accept the opportunity. We don't allow ourselves to get to game day. We take ourselves out of the game, off the field, and out of the stadium, weeks before the game is even scheduled to start. We allow that nasty little monster in our heads to take over. You might know exactly what I mean.

There are times when we may regret not taking a new role or job or not making a different decision—this is not uncommon. When we let self-doubt, negativity, and the fear of the unknown hold us in place, however, it is a problem, even though, as human beings, we are wired for stasis (desiring to stay the same). That is a survival mechanism. It is our minds trying to protect us.

You must challenge this feeling and push forward. Allow yourself to go for it. Do your analysis, and determine if it is really what you want to do. If it is, put your foot on the gas pedal. Here's the thing: when I have been in this type of situation, but I decided to go against that little monster that was screaming, "No! Don't do it," I found myself thinking—after the decision was made and months into the role—*What was I worried about? I've got this. I am good enough to do this.*

Well, you've got this. You deserve the role or opportunity. Don't take anything less. You can handle anything that is thrown at you. Map out your strategy, build your ninety-day plan, and just go for it.

SETTING YOURSELF FREE

> No man is an island entire of itself, every man is
> a piece of the continent, a part of the main.
> —John Donne

Setting yourself free might be easier said than done, of course. It's easy to say, "Don't think negative; think positive!" Negative thinking has its uses; it's important to look at things with a critical eye. Looking at things critically helps us to see where improvements need to be made. The trick is in seeing things that need to be improved only as they are, without exaggerating them. So how do we do this?

Often, we can't do this on our own. It helps to have someone else to help us talk things through or act as a sounding board. All good writers have beta readers or editors whom they trust to tell them if what they have written is good and where it can be improved. All good businesspeople have trusted advisers who can tell them which ideas will work and which ones need working on. Athletes have coaches; artists have mentors.

No matter how independent you are, you can't do things entirely on your own—you will only ever be able to see out of your own eyes. You need other people to help break you out of your own patterns of thinking and to help you see from other perspectives.

In order to fly solo, you first have to fly with help. Your first parachute jump is always taken when tethered to someone who has done it before. Your first takeoff and landing in an airplane always has a flight instructor with her hands on a second set of controls.

There is a reason why doctors and lawyers have to go to continuing-education classes each year. Even though they may have decades of experience in a particular field, it doesn't hurt to have a refresher course. Sometimes things change, and they aren't aware of the change. Sometimes things change, and you aren't aware of the change because you have been stuck inside your own head, spiraling inside your own thought patterns.

You may or may not accept everything that everyone else says. You don't have to accept every piece of advice that is offered. Sometimes, someone else's perspective only serves to show you that yours was right to begin with.

You may have other methods of getting out of your own head. There is no absolute right or wrong with this. Sometimes, just forgetting about what you are fretting about by watching a funny or suspenseful movie is the way to do it. Perhaps kickboxing or a night out with your friends works best for you. The only universal truth is that you must be self-aware enough to know when you are in your head, in that negative spiral of thoughts.

It's a cliché to say you're running around in circles and getting nowhere. Your thoughts can run around in circles, just like your body can. More often than not, the more your thoughts circle, the more negative they become. You need someone or something to break into that circle and interrupt the pattern. Get out of your head, and get some perspective. You will find—not you *may* find; you *will* find—that you are a whole lot better than you thought you were.

Box Thoughts

1. Do you frequently find yourself on a Ferris wheel that never stops?
2. How much time do you spend in your head?
3. Are you taking yourself out of the game before it starts?

CHAPTER II

Celebrate You

IN THE PAST TWO CHAPTERS, WE TALKED ABOUT WHAT TO DO when we feel stuck, but we aren't always going to feel stuck. Sometimes—most of the time, even—things will go well. We may be making progress slowly, or we may be whizzing along. As long as we are taking action with intention, in alignment with our values and beliefs, in concert with our hearts, minds, and spirits, we are on the road to success.

Along this road, we may feel like we have a great deal of momentum, and we don't want to stop. We don't want to take any breaks until we reach the goalpost. Then, when we reach the goalpost, we move the goalpost a little bit farther down the road. "I can't stop now," we might say to ourselves. "I've got too much momentum! Celebrating now is too much like counting my chickens before they hatch. I must wait until I've completed everything. Then I'll stop and really celebrate."

Having this kind of mind-set is dangerous and somewhat idiotic. If you are continuously doing and not taking the time to recognize that movement forward is worthy of celebrating, you are missing the most important ingredient. If you want to continue working toward the big things in life, you will have to learn to celebrate the small things along the way. The problem is that we get so wrapped up in what others will think about us, that if we take just a moment, our minds do what our minds do—tell us all of the reasons why we shouldn't celebrate. In many instances, it is our own doing that does us in. It drives us to a breaking point—and then, where are we?

We are left complaining that life has dished us the worst hand, when only a month ago, we were on the top of the world. How is it that we hit one wall and forget all of the walls we busted down to get to the one we just hit? We are resisting what is natural—celebrating. Think about it. If you have a puppy and are teaching it to go potty outside, you reward it with a treat. If you are like me, you make a really big deal out of it too.

We do the same thing with babies. We can't resist making a big deal out of one little accomplishment, such as their first steps. It didn't matter that the step was wobbly or that they fell; what mattered was that they did it. We naturally celebrate that by making it a big deal.

Why have we stopped doing that, somewhere along the way? What makes us feel that we have to wait to hit a big milestone? Why do we get so busy with the everyday grind that we don't take the time to drink the lemonade?

WHY CELEBRATE?

Celebrating has so many mental and physical benefits that we don't even realize the magnitude of something so simple. Something magical happens when celebrate. Our bodies and minds change because it heightens our feel-good gene. When this happens, our bodies release endorphins, which are responsible for aiding our ability to withstand the stress and pain that comes with everyday life. Our bodies also release oxytocin, which creates trust and strengthens relationships; dopamine, which motivates us but also allows us to pay attention to critical tasks; and serotonin, which adds focus. These neurotransmitters allow us to reduce stress and be happier. This combination is better than anything in the world, if you learn how to regularly activate them. Here are seven reasons why you need to celebrate:

1. It reminds you to be grateful for the things and people in your life, as well as what you have worked so hard for.
2. It reminds you to enjoy your journey—you likely are so focused on the goals and outcomes that you forget the beautiful road you have traveled.
3. It increases your capacity for joy and happiness, to have a better outlook, and to not beat yourself up, day after day.
4. It fills your need for that much-wanted approval, that pat on the back, that accolade for a job well done.
5. It recognizes action, regardless of the results, when you think about all the things you have done.
6. It allows you to have a say in how you feel, versus letting others tell us.
7. It builds confidence and momentum because you're self-motivated by those little accomplishments along the way.

On top of all of the hard work, we all deserve to be celebrated, appreciated, and acknowledged. We need to celebrate who we are every minute, every hour, every day. There is no better time than now.

WHY NOW?

There are good reasons why you should stop now and take the time to celebrate your current accomplishments. Celebration doesn't end with just you. Celebration among teams increases team loyalty, cohesiveness, and productivity. If you use the same celebration mind-set, remember it is contagious, so spread it like your spreading smooth peanut butter. Create a culture of celebration in your workplace. Acknowledge the people around you. Share those much-needed words of encouragement for you and others. Share your inner world and sense of reality, and find a way to be open to receive. Just like you broke your ultimate goal down into micro-goals, you need to break your celebrations down into micro-celebrations. If you wait until you have finished everything, there will be too much work and not enough joy—too many sticks and not enough carrots.

You have accomplished something, even if you haven't accomplished everything. Don't get so caught up in what you are doing that you can't take a moment to celebrate the simple victory of progress. Even if you haven't reached any goalposts, the act of putting one foot in front of the other and continuing down the road toward your goal is something, in and of itself, worth celebrating.

Rewarding yourself for your progress is one way of knocking yourself out of those negative thought patterns we talked about in chapter 10. If you only think about what is left to do and that you haven't finished, it's no wonder you think negatively! Developing a mind-set that allows you to go after the big things means you need to make the small things count.

Remember that this is your life we are talking about, not just the next work plan or project. When you celebrate the small things, it knocks away that nagging feeling that tears away at your self-confidence. You will find that the more you celebrate, the more confident you will be. That confidence will radiate from you in an infectious manner. If you allow it to shine, it will inspire those around you to be more confident.

It is up to you to be grateful, to celebrate who you are, to celebrate your triumphs and efforts, and to give yourself that much-needed praise to infuse resilience. You deserve it. Reward yourself with an instant gratification; place a celebration chit in your box. Write it down, shout it out to the world, and rejoice. Simply, *celebrate.*

> The more you praise and celebrate your life,
> the more there is in life to celebrate.
> —Oprah Winfrey

HOW TO CELEBRATE

What does a celebration look like? It doesn't mean throwing a catered party every time you complete a micro-goal in your box. Celebrations need to be in proportion to the accomplishments. The smaller the goal, the smaller the celebration. By celebration, I simply mean allowing yourself to do the things that make you feel good and happy.

If you are a to-do–list kind of person, give yourself a micro-reward every time you cross something off your list. You might be wondering how many different ways you could celebrate. It might be allowing yourself a game of Candy Crush or a phone call with your best friend. Maybe you will get your nails done or play tennis if you complete a certain number of items. Eat a cupcake or a handful of potato chips. Drink a cup of coffee. The possibilities are endless.

You can give yourself a little gift, reward yourself with much-needed time off, post a congratulations to yourself on social media, go shopping, document it by writing a little note to yourself, get some friends together for a little gathering, take a bubble bath, or spend a few minutes a day dedicated to you for a job well done. I could go on and on. Celebrations and rewards can be personal. These alone can help motivate you to keep walking down that path when you get tired.

One of the things I did after registering a name and starting my business was to buy something that reminded of the effort that I had put in to that point. My company name is Kaleidoscope Affect, and I purchased a nice wooden-and-brass kaleidoscope to remind me of what is yet to come. It was the greatest feeling of accomplishment when it arrived, and I put it on my desk in my office. I look at it every day, and it gives me a sense of pride.

Your reward doesn't have to be costly, big, or complicated. It just needs to be simple and meaningful to you.

If you wait to celebrate, you may wait a long time. Some goals—most goals—take years to accomplish. Take pride in what you do every day, and reward yourself accordingly.

This isn't participation-trophy stuff. Don't make a big deal out of nothing. Don't reward yourself for simply showing up and doing the bare minimum to get by. Make it a real celebration of accomplishment, and make sure that the celebration fits. The trick is to make sure you pat yourself on the back as often as you chastise yourself.

We're good at beating ourselves up when we make mistakes. We're not so good at cheering for ourselves when we do something right. That's what this is about. When you have done something—crossed the final *t* and dotted the final *i*—sit back, breathe a sigh of relief, and recognize that *you have done something*. The point is not whether this is a large goal or a micro-goal. It doesn't matter how you celebrate; it doesn't matter whether it is big or small. What matters is that you just celebrate.

Box Thoughts

1. Are you giving yourself time to smell the roses?
2. Do you celebrate the small successes?
3. What are three ways you can work celebrating *you* into your daily habits?

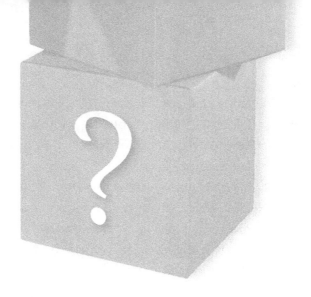

CHAPTER 12

How to Design Your Box

Our lives without purpose are similar to empty boxes.

THROUGHOUT THIS BOOK, WE'VE TALKED ABOUT OUR INTEN-
tions, values, beliefs, and actions. We have talked about being
more intentional and creating alignment in our daily lives. I've
asked you to look deep within yourself to learn who you are,
fundamentally, to make sure that you're assessing your values
and beliefs to ensure they represent your best self. Keeping in
mind the Box Theory is much larger than your goals and dreams.
Realize that you must put in the work before you see the results.
Think about everything we've covered; you now have the power
to design the life you want. It all starts with designing or selecting
your box.

Imagine how you see yourself. What visual image do you draw
up? Is there a way for you to transpose this to your physical box? If
so, what would your box look like? Can you see it? Can you select

or design something that speaks to you, that is about you, and is you? It all starts with visualizing your future self. You need to be able to appreciate and be grateful for where you are today because that empowers you to move forward.

Start by thinking about your achievements and the lessons you've learned that you want to take forward. I am also asking you to change your mind-set, here and now. It all starts with to-day. This is about training yourself—mind, body, and spirit—to manifest your dreams. It is creating a daily habit of being intentional about what you do to move you forward. Build a habit that is about you, and create the life you want. It is about your actions and behaviors and whether they serve you well. Think about those things that trigger good behavior and bad behavior. It is about making a promise to yourself on a daily basis. Think about your intentions from the start and determine why you do what you do. It is about questioning your long-held beliefs and values to determine if they are holding you back. It is also about building in the much-needed time to recover, replenish, and simply celebrate the small things.

All of this goes into the design of your box. Your box is representative of your individual goals but also your intentions and your way of being. You've got to visualize your box as clear as a sunny day. Once you've thought hard about what goes inside your box—the big things and the little things, the parts that make up the whole—it will be time to get down to brass tacks.

Up until now, we've been talking about the box as metaphor, not necessarily an actual box but a box as a concept. Now, I'd like you to get an actual box that you can use. Just like your metaphorical box, it doesn't matter what kind of box it is. It can be a shoebox that you repurpose. It can be a box made of fine china or silver. You might prefer a fancy box that you've decorated. It only matters that it suits your vision, as we've discussed.

Using Symbolic Objects to Fill Your Box

Now that you have your box, it is time to lay out your dreams and goals. While these may be larger, more elaborate things, you will eventually need to break them down into more bite-size pieces. This process is similar to (but not exactly like) a vision board. The two are complementary and can be used together. You may find that using symbolic objects on your vision board to represent large goals and then writing down the micro-goals on your chits focused on accomplishing those large goals reflected on your vision board. I personally like to use both.

I have a vision board with big goals and dreams on it. These are things that take years to achieve, such as paying off my house and building my business. In my box are smaller, more realistic goals, such as getting my professional certified coach certificate from the International Coaching Federation or getting third-party qualification for a woman-owned small business. Because of where I am in my journey, these were things that I could put into play for completion within 90 to 120 days. One of my larger goals was writing this book, but along the way, I set smaller more achievable goals to accomplish this. I celebrated finishing every chapter. So you see, you don't need to limit yourself to the types of things you may be working toward.

Just as you might want to take a peek at a vision board to remind you of where you want to go, it sometimes helps to have a physical reminder of the chits in your box. The key is moving from the metaphorical to the theoretical. Having a real, tangible box with real, tangible chits in it that represent goals and dreams can make achieving them seem more real.

Of course, you can't fit an actual value or belief in a box. These are concepts, not things, but you can put a chit with a word, phrase, or even a symbolic object in the box that represents these things. The idea is that you can open your box, see the items you have placed in it, and pick them up and feel them to remind you of what you have accomplished and what is to come.

Sometimes, it can be easy to figure out what you're going to focus on, and other times, it may not be. You do need to get consistent, make this a ritual, and focus. By doing this, you will gain clarity on what you really want in life. My own perspective changed when I reached a major goal. For the longest time, on my vision board was my graduation for my PhD. At that time, I was not using the box theory, but I was using micro-goals as the mechanism to help me move closer to achieving that goal, which took seven years. My celebration for that event was being able to walk across the stage to get my degree. This was a major celebration for me because it was the first time, ever, that I had walked in a graduation. This is a good example of how personal this is and the impact it can make on your life.

You might want to use a combination of chits and picture representations in your box. As a reminder, the chits are little slips of paper with goals or micro-goals on them. Maybe they contain a statement of belief or have a value written on them. They can be fancy pieces of paper with calligraphy written on them, or they can be scraps of paper with something scribbled on them. The point is not whether the paper is pretty, plain, or decorative or whether the handwriting is fancy, but that it is reflective of the it represents rather than just words on pieces of paper.

Think about your career goals, health and well-being, love life, family life, personal relationships, continuing education, and other things that you want to focus on. Create your big goal and your micro-goals. Write them down. Put them in your box.

Is there something that has great meaning to you? Do you treasure the first dollar you ever earned? Is it a letter from your grandmother, telling you that she knew you could be a success? Maybe it's your hard-earned college diploma that represents your getting a better job, or maybe it's a movie-theater ticket stub from an important date with someone you want to build a life with. Whatever gives you inspiration and encouragement, put it in your box.

The box itself can become significantly meaningful and important if it truly represents you and your uniqueness. I think about my grandmother's silver box and how meaningful it was—and is—to me.

What Can You Get Out of Filling Up the Box?

> While a box has perceived physical limitations,
> it is our thinking that actually limits us.

Why are we bothering to do this? Isn't it enough that we know what our goals and dreams are, without going through this process? Isn't our time better spent actually doing the work, instead of doing this visualization stuff?

Visualization itself is one of the most powerful exercises you can do on a daily basis. Use your mind to see the end, and use the box theory to carry out putting the pieces together. There is benefit in putting your goals into our boxes. When we feel lost or as if we have lost the path, it may be helpful to go to our respective boxes and reflect on our goals, why we put them there, and why we are on the path in the first place. It's one thing to have a goal in your mind; it is quite another to be able to pick it up and touch it.

Have a symbolic representation inside your box that you can pick up and touch in a manner that helps you to see if it's coming to realization. Let's say, for example, you want to open a restaurant to showcase all the recipes that your grandmother taught you. There are a million things you have to do first. You have to finish culinary school. You have to write your business plan, find a location, get investors, build out the space, hire wait staff and cooks, write the menu and replicable recipes, buy the appliances and pots and pans, get an accounting system in place and a way to take credit cards, design the signs outside, and figure out a marketing plan—and that's just for starters! It can feel overwhelming. But if you open your box and pull out your chit with the restaurant name on it or a picture that you put in to highlight what your end result will be, that is very powerful. This will remind you that it takes you a step at a time—micro-goal by micro-goal as small steps—toward your larger passion.

Even the act of putting micro-goals or accomplishments in your box can be inspiring. Each time you place an object in the box, even something small, you know that you are building toward something. As the box fills with your goals, make sure that you take out the completed ones to celebrate. It is about putting in to get out, similar to paying yourself, except you are making a payment on your future. You don't need to fill every square inch of space inside your box, as long as you are working toward intentional goals, intentional growth. Every chit, every symbol, is a part of your planned goals and represents a piece of your life and a step along your path that is well thought out. You can actually see your plans take shape and your dreams come true.

USING ACTIONS, BEHAVIORS, AND PROMISES TO BUILD AND DESIGN YOUR BOX TO ACHIEVE SUCCESS

You don't have to be an artist or a design expert to make the most beautiful, wonderful box in the world. Your box doesn't have to be beautiful to anyone but you. Your box doesn't need to be made with perfect proportions or artistic lines. What is important is that your box is made with the intention of changing your actions and behaviors and living up to your promises to yourself and others.

This box alone will not make you successful; it is the effort that you put in to moving your life forward in an intentional way, using the box theory and micro-goal concept. You don't need to design and build it with mathematical precision. Instead, you need to build it with pure intention. You need to fill it with values that reflect who you are and that will be productive. You need to construct it with actions and behaviors that work for you, not against you.

When you say you are going to build your box, you need to build your box. Keep your word and your promises to yourself and to everyone around you. Remember that the box is the physical representation of your life. You get to choose, design, build, and put into it what matters in living your very best life. You won't achieve it all at once, but through time, you can have it all, just not at the same time.

Design your box with these parameters in mind. As long as you follow these parameters every time you lift the lid of the box, sift through the goals, pull out the chit that is completed, and celebrate your completion, you *will* achieve success.

ABOUT THE AUTHOR

DR. LINDA L. SINGH IS A LEADERSHIP EXPERT WITH MORE THAN thirty-eight years of experience working with individuals and teams in overcoming challenges and obstacles impacting their forward progression. Singh is the author of *Moments of Choice: My Path to Leadership* and has appeared on the Today Show for her history-making leadership team. She is a combat veteran, a wife, and mother of two daughters.

CPSIA information can be obtained
at www.ICGtesting.com
Printed in the USA
BVHW030202091120
592835BV00009B/185